UTILIZING THIS TEXT

Together with the workshop, this guide, **_The Enneagram Personality Styles,_** is a powerful tool for individuals *and* helping professionals in private practice. Therapists, spiritual directors, life coaches, pastors, and leaders remark on the effective way this material is laid out as they assist their clients/directees in the work of transformation. This book explains in accessible terms what the Enneagram is and how to utilize it with each personality style in discovering the essence of the human person and assisting persons in the opening to grace.

"Clare Loughrige's Enneagram materials have been invaluable to me as a spiritual director. Her knowledge of and insights into the Enneagram have helped me to understand this valuable instrument in ways I previously had not. Again and again, I find that when I use her materials with others, paths to freedom in Christ are discovered in ways not previously seen. Plus, hearing Clare teach on the Enneagram makes the material come alive even more!" —**Mary Albert Darling author, Associate Professor of Communication, Adjunct, Masters in Spiritual Formation and Leadership Chair, Christian Perspective in the Liberal Arts (CPLA), Spring Arbor University**

Endorsements for _THE ENNEAGRAM PERSONALITY STYLES,_ AND _MOTIONS OF THE SOUL_ Workshops and Retreats-

Clare is a very energetic and interactive speaker. She has creatively combined some traditional practices of spirituality, particularly Ignatian spiritual practices, with the Enneagram spectrum of personality styles. You will find her presentations engaging, thoughtful, and useful. —**Jerome Wagner, Ph.D., author of** Nine Lenses on the World: the Enneagram Perspective **and** The Enneagram Spectrum of Personality Styles

It's my privilege to endorse Enneagram workshops presented by Rev. Clare Loughrige for the Spiritual Care Consultants [SCC] staff. These workshops have given me a way to understand myself as SCC's leader and the dynamics of the team I lead. We have grown in empathy and compassion for the people we minister to as a result of [our] own self-knowledge. This has been a great investment in the SCC staff. I would recommend these workshops for any business or ministry. —**Gale Kragt, Ph.D., president of Spiritual Care Consultants**

We are very grateful for Clare's facilitation, teaching and the understanding she imparted to us at Family Tree Medical Practice with the Enneagram workshop. The Lord has blessed her with many talents, and she is sharing them to impact others. In this case, not only our team but the patients we serve. Thank you. —**R. Troy Carlson, M.D., Family Tree Medical Practice (Hastings MI)**

West Michigan Wesleyan Pastors' "41 Hours" Retreat

I wholeheartedly recommend Clare Loughrige to you. I have invited Clare to speak in both a small group (approximately 25) and a larger group (more than 200), and in each setting, we have found her presentations to be engaging, insightful, and meaningful for each participant. Clare knows how to keep an audience's attention using the right amount of humor and pertinent examples while presenting the material in a fast-paced manner. I believe your organization will benefit both from the Enneagram and the way Clare presents it. —**Rev. Chris Conrad, district superintendent, West Michigan District, Wesleyan Church**

- *"Great information to take home and apply"*
- *"We will use this!"*
- *"Great tool for ministry and marriage"*
- *"I was very impressed. Provided great conversation with my wife and with our church staff that attended."*
- *"Wish it could have been longer"*
- *"A new approach for me and opened up a lot of good discussion about the staff and at my church"*
- *"New insights, and it's taught me never to hire staff without going through some sort of 'personality' test to ensure compatibility. It also really helped my wife and I understand more about each other. Brilliant! Clare was extremely articulate and a great communicator."*

© *The Enneagram Personality Styles: A Tool for Self-Knowledge and Spiritual Transformation*, Clare Loughrige 2016

Graphic Artist: Stacey Livingston, *slivingston@ccmonline.org*
Edited by Samuel Ogles, SD *(SamuelOgles.com)*

First Printing, 2007. © All Rights Reserved.

Because this material is original and some of it is used with the permission of other sources, do not make copies of this material without permission from the author.

®CSR PUBLISHING 2016

TABLE OF CONTENTS

	Page
Personality Styles Diagram	4
Harmony Triads for Integration and Discernment	5
Welcome Home - Enneagram Basics	6
Enneagram's History	9
Enneagram-Type Descriptive Paragraphs	11
The Centers	14
Triad Center Prayer Descriptions	16
iEnneagram Diagram – Little Examen	17
The Powerful Person - Type 8	18
The Peaceful Person - Type 9	22
The Good Person - Type 1	26
The Loving Person - Type 2	30
The Effective Person - Type 3	34
The Original Person - Type 4	38
The Wise Person - Type 5	42
The Loyal Person - Type 6	46
The Joyful Person - Type 7	50

Reflection Exercises

Presence and Non-Presence: A Reflection Exercise	54
Psalm 139 True Self/False Self Reflections	58
Spiritual Practice of Transformation	60
Reflections with a Spiritual Friend	61
Enneagram Courses and Certification Program	62
Sources and Resources	65

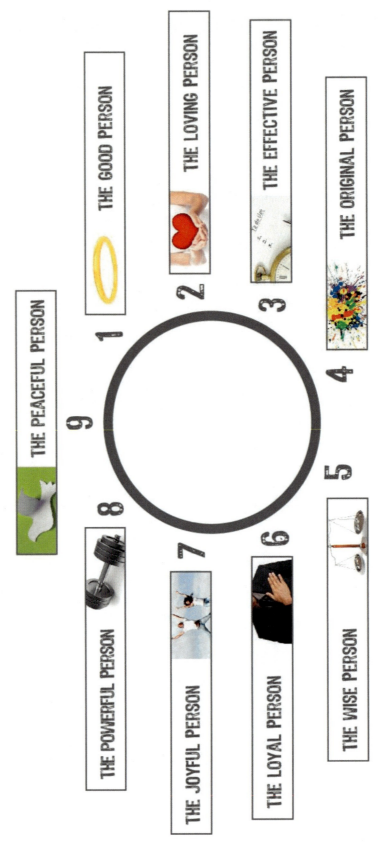

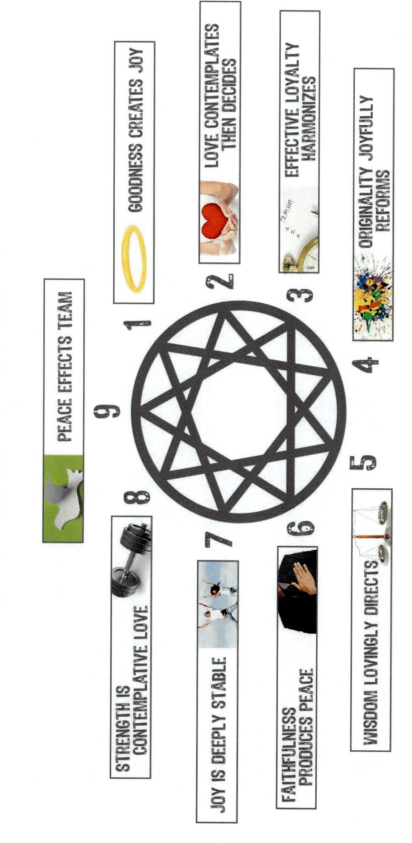

WELCOME HOME

> *"With God's help, I shall become myself."*
> —Søren Kierkegaard

Becoming ourselves is the unique work of the Enneagram. Many personality tests describe who we are, but the Enneagram calls us back to the original intent of our <u>one and only life</u>.

The Enneagram Personality Styles is a psychological-spiritual system for mapping the nine personalities. This map allows an individual to name their story and be aware of the way that story is moving toward salvation and integration or toward disintegration.

> *"By salvation I mean not barely according to the vulgar notion deliverance from hell*
> *or going to heaven but a present deliverance from sin,*
> *a restoration of the soul to its primitive health, its original purity,*
> *a recovery of the divine nature,*
> *the renewal our souls after the image of God*
> *in righteousness and true holiness in justice, mercy, and truth."*
> —John Wesley

The Enneagram helps us see the primitive health and purity of our soul and describes how to recover that purity. This tool can bring awareness to everyday life, keeping us in touch with that which brings us a blessed life. Staying awake and aware of the way we live is both liberating and empowering.

When awareness becomes regular and intentional, we let go of anxiety, guilt, fear, and shame and virtues flow through us. This tool releases old patterns of reaction and brings movement rather than "stuckness."

ENNEAGRAM BASICS
The name "Enneagram" comes from two Greek words: *ennea* meaning "nine" and *gram* meaning "points." The Enneagram is a model about nine distinct and interrelated personality types, or nine ways of seeing and experiencing the world.

George Box said, "All models are wrong, but some are useful." This system is more than useful; it can transform your life. The Enneagram provides an explanation of what the Bible describes about "the fall of man" and the sins that have tripped us up since then. Once we discover how we have fallen, this map illuminates new choices on how we would like to journey as a "new creation" from here.

The Enneagram also gives a description of psychological filters or blindness that have developed as our coping strategies. We all take reality in through a filter, our perceived reality. Discovering that "we don't see things as they are, but we see things as we are" can heal our sight.

Richard Rohr describes it this way:

> *All problems are interpreted today psychologically, but the real solutions are spiritual. There is a primary blindness in each of us, an addiction. What we are addicted to is self and protecting that self. Until that egocentricity is broken, we will read all of life through personal self-interest. It is the shape and name of our primary flaw. This typology uses nine basic shapes to describe this flaw, a primary ill perception that we're addicted to.* ("Enneagram: The Discernment of Spirits," Richard Rohr MP3)

This flaw is called "false self" compulsion or "old man." The system can help us unmask the false self and bring that false self to the transforming power of God. That is the goal of the Enneagram.

When a person is humbled by the truth of who they are, both their exquisite essence and unconscious compulsion, one can bring intention to that awareness and experience the transforming grace of God. The truth will set us free, and it will also humble and disturb us! Unlike other personality typologies, this model sees the shadow or wounded personality as the false self and the true self as being your God-image or the Essence or God. The work of this system is to "become yourself."

The system is not intended to put anyone in a box. No individual is one type alone. We are made up of a dominant type, and two numbers on either side called "wings" and a Harmony Triad, which point to the way of deformation/disintegration along with transformation/integration. This system, therefore, is very individually specific, based on the individual journey and each one's willingness to yield to God.

We will use many characteristics of the personality in detailing each type's style. In describing the journey of the soul, we will unpack each type's **"true self/false self"** dynamics.

True Self (essence) emerges from union with God and has nothing to do with performance. It was the non-acquired self. It is our essence, our reflection of the God-image. The truest thing about us is that we are God's temple, a home for God. Virtues describe the true self.

False Self (compulsive, old nature-self) is the psychological self that is made up of past and present, the family of origin issues, nature, nurture, and free will. It is your false self, the adapted coping style of self. The vices describe the false self.

Transformation (redemption) is bringing the wounded false self to God and being healed by the same thing that has wounded you (much like inoculation).

CLOUDY WITH A CHANCE OF MEATBALLS

Have you seen the movie *Cloudy with a Chance of Meatballs*? It is a classic story of how too much of a good thing becomes a bad thing. A boy makes a machine that can rain food from the sky to save an island that has lived on sardines only and before you know it they are being attacked by an overabundance of meatballs and all the other good food. Just like the movie or the weather, any given day you could show up as "true-self with a chance of false self" or "false self with an intermittent chance of true-self."

On our best day, we are a mixed bag of motivations and possible reactions. Developing awareness, of all parts of our human condition, has a transformational muscle.

WISDOM SAYINGS THAT CALL US TO BE AWARE AND THEN MOVE US FROM AWARENESS TO SPIRITUAL TRANSFORMATION

"All wisdom, if it is to be thought genuine, consists almost entirely of two parts: the knowledge of God and of ourselves." —John Calvin

"People travel to wonder at the height of mountains, at the huge waves of the sea, at the long courses of rivers, at the circular motions of the stars and they pass by themselves without wondering." —Augustine

"I met the enemy, and the enemy is me." —Unknown

"The sinner is actually one who does not love himself/herself enough." —Julian of Norwich

"If you do not transform your wounds, you will transmit them." —Richard Rohr

"If men knew themselves, God would heal and pardon them." —Blaise Pascal

"Spiritual transformation is the process by which Christ is formed in us for the glory of God, the abundance of our own lives, and for the sake of others." —Ruth Haley Barton

Each of these "wisdom sayings" builds on the next, taking us from an invitation to know God and self—including facing the beauty and grime of our lives—to the transformation that exalts God and forms our lives for the good of ourselves and the world. These building blocks lay the groundwork for ***The Enneagram of Personality Styles: A Tool for Self-Knowledge and Spiritual Transformation***.

The Enneagram's History

There is some dispute about the roots of the Enneagram. Jerry Wagner, clinical psychologist at the Institute of Pastoral Studies at Loyola University Chicago, says, "Some authors believe they have found variations of the Enneagram symbol in the sacred geometry of the Pythagoreans who 4000 years ago were interested in the deeper meaning and significance of numbers. This line of mystical mathematics was passed on through Plato, his disciple Plotinus, and subsequent neo-Platonists." (www.enneagramspectrum.com).

Richard Rohr has done a comprehensive study in the Enneagram's roots in his book *The Enneagram: a Christian Perspective*. Through this research, we find that the Enneagram's roots can be traced back to the desert monk, Evagrius Ponticus, (AD 399) and the Franciscan monk, Ramon Llull, in the 12th and 13th centuries. Ponticus wrote about how the desert fathers and mothers worked to help people grow spiritually.

Both Ponticus and Llull saw patterns in the way people viewed themselves and life. The patterns developed into systems for conversion and formation. Ponticus started with the seven capital sins (as defined by the desert mothers and fathers) to create the basis of the "shadow side" of the Enneagram. Ponticus added "deceit" to make eight and the final "compulsion of fear" was added at some point which is unknown to make nine.

Centuries later, Ramon Llull took eight missionary trips to the Muslim world (Afghanistan, Iran, Iraq, and Syria) in his work as an evangelist. He used Ponticus' work as an evangelical tool. Llull produced an extensive work on life patterns. Although the Sufi schools eventually adopted the work, the Enneagram seems to have gotten lost to the west. His work included the use of geometric forms to map out various patterns, which is similar to what is called the Harmony Triads, represented by three triangles. This pattern is the wisdom of my work on the ©*iEnneagram, Motions of the Soul* and what is found in this guide.

It appears that further discovery was done in the Sufi schools of spiritual direction, and the Enneagram returned to the Christian west in the late 1960s by Jesuit-trained Oscar Ichazo. Ichazo taught the system to his student Claudio Naranjo, a psychiatrist. Naranjo taught the Enneagram in Berkley, California, in the 1970s, having added his psychological knowledge. Robert Ochs then taught the Enneagram with a combination of spiritual direction and psychological understanding to a group of Jesuits who, after testing and theological examination, began to use this tool in spiritual direction and retreats. Initially, the Enneagram was intended to be taught in the oral tradition but finally found its way into print in the 1980s by people like Helen Palmer, Don Riso, Richard Rohr, Pat O'Leary, and others.

Through Ochs, the Enneagram was introduced to various Christian communities where Jerome Wagner (the psychologist mentioned above) learned the Enneagram. I am a certified teacher under Jerome Wagner. My work has also been accepted by Wagner's First Analysis Institute of Integrative Studies.* The institute's website states, *"For over 20 years the First Analysis Institute and Loyola University [Chicago] has recognized experts from the fields of psychology, psychiatry, organizational development, business, education, spirituality, theology, et al, to explore the rules and applications of the Personality Enneagram."* *integrativestudies.com

The Enneagram industry continues to grow in the secular world. The disciplines of business and psychology have taken it to new heights. However, those of us that see this as a tool of spiritual transformation are saddened about the Enneagram being trivialized into mere self-development. The power of the Enneagram is as a sacred tool to assist us in being conformed to the image of Christ. In its pure form, the Enneagram assists Christ followers in discovering interior freedom. It offers knowledge to assist us in moving from compulsive living to contemplative living, from information to transformation, from vice to virtue, and from "False Self" to "True Self."

DISCOVERING YOUR ENNEAGRAM TYPE The test below is a self-administered test based on reading nine descriptive paragraphs and choosing the one or two that most resemble you. **For comprehensive testing, go to enneagramspectrum.com**

Pray
Find a quiet and comfortable place free from distractions and just breathe. Quiet down any anxiety within by breathing in the reality that, in the beginning, you were masterfully created by God, and anything you experience through this personality instrument is for your blessing. Pray a simple prayer that can open you to see what you haven't been able to see before. A simple prayer like, "Jesus I want to see. Holy Spirit illuminate my heart, mind, and instincts in these moments set apart to see myself, led by love."

The nine paragraphs reflect each type's overall filter or view of life. All nine paragraphs may describe you to some degree but choose the one or ones that are most like you. When you choose a paragraph or two, they won't be "100% you," but that paragraph will be more like you than the other seven or eight. Write down those like-paragraph numbers. Remember there isn't a "better" number, so be as honest as you are able about who you are. Don't choose who you wish you were. (For comprehensive testing, go to enneagramspectrum.com)

Enneagram-Type Descriptive Paragraphs
Read and Reflect

I am very conscientious and want to be good. I look for ways to live correctly and help others around me live properly. Some people say I am a perfectionist or anal-retentive. I have a strong inner critic or voice that directs me with what I "should do" or "ought to do." I tend to "should" all over myself. I try to avoid showing anger and being vulnerable. Some people think I am controlling, but I have high internal standards for what is right. I can spot when something is wrong and will work hard to perfect it. I enjoy seeing something done the right way, and I will put aside my needs to see a job get done perfectly. I will do my very best to see things well ordered and finished. I have a hard time when people don't have that same standard for their work. When people expect a hand-out or are irresponsible, it makes me angry. Fairness and correctness are at the top of my list. If it's not right, I will reform it, clean it, restructure it, and do whatever it takes to make it better. (1)

I am a friendly, self-sacrificing person. I love to see what a person needs and then be the one to give it to them. I am very intuitive and sensitive to others. I have a strong desire to be loved and appreciated for what I do. I would like to do more for people than I do and will go above and beyond the call of duty. It comes very naturally for me to give of myself. I am usually busy taking care of others and unaware of my needs. I am not good at saying no. I don't like to disappoint people, so I end up putting more energy into loving others than loving myself. Some people may think I am clingy or possessive. It saddens me if people think I'm trying to control them through my caring. I like people to see me as cheerful, self-sufficient, warmhearted, and sacrificing. I work very hard to make real heartfelt relationships happen. I am nurturing and empathetic but sometimes can hurt myself by being "martyr-like." When I am hurt, the words "after all I've done for you!" have been known to come out of my mouth. When I am offended, I can get vindictive or take revenge. (2)

I am a productive achiever. I see someone or something, and I look at how I can make it, or them, succeed. I like things to work and be productive. You might say I grease the wheels to make stuff happen. I am diplomatic and image conscious. I like to shine, look competent, and fruitful. Life is a series of tasks, goals, and accomplishments. I do things efficiently and sometimes at a high rate of speed. I do everything to avoid failure. My identity can come too much from what I do or accomplish. Sometimes I think my value comes from doing and not being. I set aside my emotions or needs to get a job done. I like to be on top and am irritated with people when they slow the process down because of incompetence. Slowing down the pace is very uncomfortable for me because I feel unproductive, and that feels like a failure. I am a good leader but also a great team player. To succeed when I am under pressure, I tend to cut corners and do things in the most efficient way even if it calls for being deceitful and superficial. When I'm healthy, I am a great motivating leader who helps people become the best they can be. (3)

I am a sensitive person with powerful feelings and a vibrant, creative imagination. I feel (or have felt in the past) as though I am not like other people and that nobody understands me. That's because I seek depth, meaning, and authenticity of feeling and self-expression in my life. Beauty, love, sorrow, and pain touch me deeply. Looking at a piece of art or a sunset or listening to music can be a religious experience for me. I love aesthetics and can change my clothing or environment over and over again to reflect what I feel inside. Some people see me as being overly dramatic, but I see life in the sixth dimension. I long for authentic relationships and rarely find them. I have always been in pursuit of emotional connectedness and feel I will never have it. My life always seems like there is something more, better, more fulfilling than I have, and I will keep reaching to attain it. Sometimes I am envious of what I perceive others to have that I don't, and this can lead to melancholy or depression. I am introspective, creative, intuitive, and in touch with the hidden depths of life and emotions. (4)

I am a quiet, cerebral observer. I desire to gain knowledge and observe life at a distance. I value my space and my privacy. I am an analytical person and want to be safe and in control of my feelings. I do not like to be in the middle of things but enjoy observing and categorizing those that are. I am calm, perceptive, curious, and insightful when I am at my best. I sometimes feel socially awkward. I enjoy an experience later when I'm thinking about it more than when I'm actually in it. I can be withholding and arrogant. I avoid rude, loud, or demanding people who express strong feelings. I don't like people to expect me to share my feelings; I like to experience my feelings alone. I do not like large crowds and don't have a strong need to be with people. I love to gather more and more information. When I am under extreme stress, I get agitated and sometimes think that someone has either moved my things or done something else to interrupt my work. My mental life is very active, and my emotional life is very private. (5)

I am motivated by a desire for safety and security. I am a loyal person who longs for a sense of belonging. I have a constant background of anxiety due to my vivid imagination. I wonder what might go wrong and don't want to be defenseless. When I perceive something is dangerous or harmful, it is as real to me as if danger or harm were happening. I can be fearful of dangerous situations and withdraw or I can confront them head on. I am always aware, even subconsciously aware, of what might go wrong. I tend to be suspicious, so I think about who can be trusted or not trusted. I look for the hidden meanings and messages and am sometimes known to play the devil's advocate. Tradition and or stability are vital to me. I don't readily trust authority but don't necessarily want to be the authority. My friends can count on me to be loyal to them to the end. When I find something to believe in, I am loyal to people, systems, organizations, and traditions, sometimes to a fault. (6)

I view life as an adventure. I want to be on the go, experiencing new and exciting things. People say I am the life of a party. I am a seeker of excitement. I love enthusiasm and spontaneity. When doing something I enjoy, I'll devote myself wholeheartedly to it. Conversely, if I don't like it or it bores me, I will look for a way out. My imagination is a non-stop playground, and I love to connect ideas and information and see how they can work together to make something new. I like to be involved at the beginning of something when things are fresh, and the playing field is wide open. I always want to move on to the next trip, the next idea, the next opportunity. When difficult things happen, I try to "change the channel" by thinking of something else or doing something else. I avoid pain at all costs. I am optimistic, and I am counting on being able to live a fun and enjoyable life. (7)

I am a person who is independent and vigorous. I like being respected for my strength and dependability. It is more important to be respected for who I am than to be liked. I am a no-nonsense go-getter who values honesty and faithfulness. I have no room for people who choose to be weak but will crusade for those who are weak with no choice. I resist following orders from people I do not agree with and will always challenge the status quo. I will defend people I care about at any cost. My opinion will be known, and my presence felt on issues that matter to me and sometimes even issues that don't matter. I am a fighter against what I consider to be unjust and am comfortable taking the lead. I am direct, confrontational, decisive, and courageous in the heat of battle and can create my wars. Some people may think I'm bossy or even manipulative, but I don't want to take anyone's power, and I don't want them to have power over me. I am known for having the last word. (8)

I am a mediator. I have a strong desire to bring peace and harmonize people to create a peace-filled and comfortable life. I accommodate others' needs and feelings quickly. I prefer to see others happy at the expense of my feelings. I am not concerned about what is important to me but what is important to everyone else in the group. I can see everyone's side in a conflict and how each one is important and needs to be considered. This consideration can make me appear too passive or indecisive, but I prefer to save decisiveness for the important issues. I keep anger in check, and I rarely display it. I am diplomatic and able to help people come to resolutions. I am adaptable, calm, nonjudgmental and supportive. I don't like confrontation and discomfort in relationships. I rarely have my agenda and am pretty adept at seeing who does. If I can see myself in all nine paragraphs, this may be my personality style. (9)

NINE TYPES FOUND IN THREE KINDS OF INTELLIGENCE: Centers or Triads

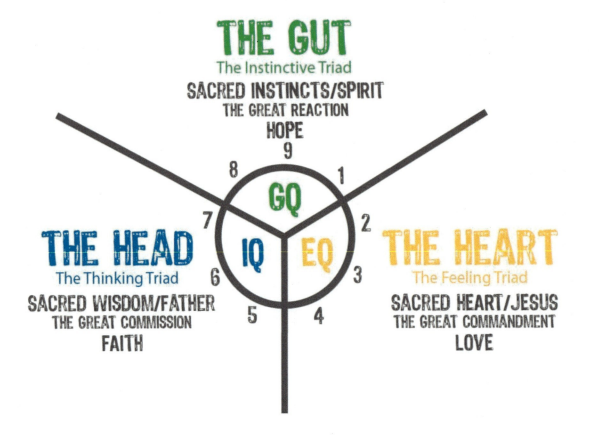

Once you discover your Enneagram Style, note where your type lands in THE TRIADS diagram. The Enneagram recognizes three different and equally important kinds of intelligence: an intelligence of the heart or feeling (types 2, 3, 4), of the head or thinking center (types 5, 6, 7), and of the body, instincts or gut (types 8, 9, 1). While all types use all three centers of intelligence, each of the triads relies especially on one over the others—either the heart, head, or body center.
(For teaching on Trinitarian wisdom and the Enneagram, refer to the ©iEnneagram: ©Motions of the Soul:© iEnneagram, Loughrige, Clare 2012.)

The Gut Triad (8, 9, 1): Instinctual or Gut Intelligence (GQ)

True Self: Types of Eight, Nine, and One perceive or filter the world through Instinctual or Gut Intelligence—GQ. They are the spaces of instincts. Sensations and body intelligence assists in developing an awareness of how much force or power to use, the will to take effective action, and a sense of grounded stability. GQ types receive energy by both the inner and the outer world.
False Self: These types get stuck in the emotion of anger. They resist being vulnerable to assure personal position or place in the world, gain comfort, or know that life is the way it "should be." Survival depends on being in control and not revealing their weaknesses to anyone. They may get stuck in converting all their feelings into anger, and then they count on this energy to produce a sense of strength and power. They get stuck in their own brand of reality of what is right and wrong and build their case and take action based on their reality. The dominant fixation is anger (repressed, expressed, or suppressed), resentment, and guilt, believing the false narrative, "I haven't done enough" or "I've had enough."

The Heart Triad (2, 3, 4): Emotional Intelligence (EQ)

True Self: The Feeling Triad—EQ types—perceive the world through a filter of Emotional Intelligence tuned into feelings and mood—EQ. Emotional intelligence also assists in developing empathy, compassion, and kindness. The people in this triad have a natural personal energy, and connection is highly valued.

False Self: Either they compare themselves with others in ways that make them feel inadequate or when they are outstanding they feel a sense of shame for making others feel inadequate. They have an obsession with feeling valued, loved, and worthy. They are unaware and do not acknowledge their personal needs. They are very "feeling" dominated, and the feelings they are dominated by are other people's feelings. Their dominant fixation is fear of humiliation and shame, believing the false narrative, "I am not enough" and "I must prove I have value."

The Head Triad (5, 6, 7): Thinking Intelligence (IQ)

True Self: The people in this triad filter the world through Mental Intelligence—IQ. Cognitive Intelligence (IQ) assists in developing insight, wisdom, and inner vision. When moved to action, they offer new ways to do things and help put dissimilar pieces together.

False Self: They may become paralyzed with fear, which causes them to withdraw into their head. They focus on strategies and beliefs that move them away from action and others. They can become gluttonous, legalistic, and possessive. To manage painful situations, minimize anxiety, or gain security and certainty, they systematize and categorize life. Their dominant fixation is fear and anxiety, believing the lie, "I don't have enough" or "I'll get what I want, whatever it takes."

TRIAD CENTER PRAYER DESCRIPTIONS

One of these centers of prayer—heart, head or body—will be your preference. Experiencing them all will be a way to go deeper in your relationship with God and your soul. *"Love the LORD your God with all your heart, with all your soul, with all your mind, and all your strength"* (Deuteronomy 6:5).

With GQ (gut center, body intel) our prayers connect us with God through the use of our hands, feet, and voice. Body prayers are on our knees, hands raised, on our feet walking or dancing, or complete stillness. In the body, we are aware of sensations. We can feel our life and reality, the power of the present moment. The body can answer the question, "How am I, and how am I being touched?" The body knows! Offering our bodies as a living sacrifice connects our lives to God.

With EQ (heart center, emotional intel) one can pray imagery prayers. Imagery prayers include reading psalms and parables with the eye and ear of the heart or using a sacred image or symbol to evoke emotion. Emotional prayers can open us to compassion and repentance. Someone said it this way, "The heart has reasons that reason knows not of." The heart can help us practice receptivity, opening us to self and others. The heart asks, "Who am I with, and what is needed?" The reality of needs and the emotions associated with them result in deepening our love for God and people.

With IQ (head center, intellectual intel) we experience God through words: memorized words, questioning words, complaining words, worshipping words, intercession, creeds, confessions, thanksgivings, reading prayers, and writing prayers. Prayers with no words—the practice of contemplation, the stillness of the mind, awareness of God's presence—all of these create the space for God to give direction and all open us to the wisdom of God. Studying the Psalms of praise, mourning, and the imprecatory Psalms lead to a wholeness and closeness to God and man's reality.

THE ©iENNEAGRAM DIAGRAM (HARMONY TRIADS)

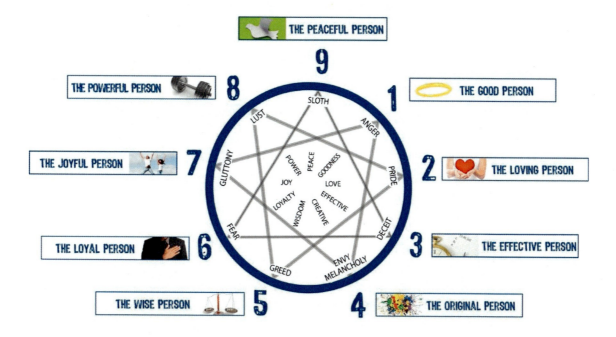

THE HARMONY TRIADS refer to **connecting the three centers of intelligence** that each of us can access. The ©iEnneagram* is about developing the awareness of the "motions of the soul." When we are aware of those motions, we bring an intentional response to that attention and life changes for ourselves and the world "God so loves." *Refer to the ©iEnneagram: Motions of the Soul. Ignatian Spirituality, Ramon Llull's diagrams and the Enneagram. ©Loughrige, Clare 2012

> *"The Enneagram of Harmony Triads are the key to development…"*
> David Daniels, M.D.

A LITTLE EXAMEN

1. What do I feel least grateful for about myself? What do I love the least? Where do I feel the absence of God's pleasure? If where you feel the absence of God is because of sin, confess this sin, ask for and receive forgiveness for missing the mark…

2. What do I feel most grateful for about myself? What do I love the most? Where do I feel the presence of God's pleasure? Now see yourself held by God in all of your gratitude…

> "Let the beloved of the LORD rest secure in him, for he shields his children all day long, and the one the LORD loves rests between his shoulders."
> Deuteronomy 33:12

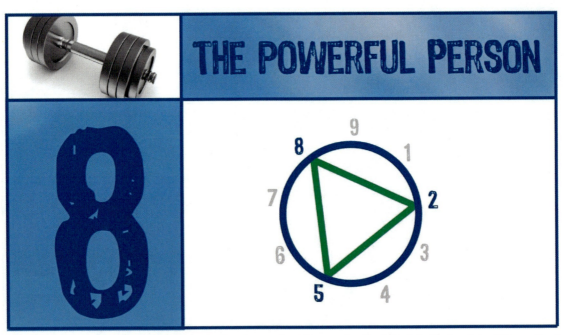

THE POWERFUL PERSON

"A father to the fatherless, a defender of widows, is God in his holy dwelling. God sets the lonely in families; he leads forth the prisoners with singing, but the rebellious live in a sun-scorched land." Psalms 68:5–6

TRUE SELF: The Powerful Person. Eights show us that God is strong. Eights are resourceful, decisive, and protective. Transforming Eights use their strength to improve others' lives, becoming noble and even heroic. Eights have a drive to feel powerful and in control over situations and their own lives. Being weak or vulnerable is avoided at all costs. They prefer respect over approval. They are earthy and worldly, and they boldly live bigger-than-life experiences. Transforming Eights, when they are living in presence and harmony with God's spirit, are self-confident, strong, protective, resourceful, and decisive. Transforming Eights use empathetic leadership, warm direction, and loving power. Holy muscle both constricts and relaxes allowing vulnerability. Centered Eights embody Sacred Strength.

FALSE SELF: Unaware Eights can be aggressive, confrontational, oppressive, self-centered, self-righteous, domineering, insensitive, and prone to excess. More and bigger is always better. They are proud and bossy, addressing injustices with their own brand of justice. Non-transforming Eights must be the boss, call the shots, direct the cruise, right the wrongs, and have to have "THE" last word. They have problems allowing themselves to trust or be close to others.

AUTHENTIC TRUE SELF: Powerful, Sacred Strength
COMPULSIVE FALSE SELF: Lustful

REDEMPTIVE VIRTUE BACK TO TRUE SELF: Innocence

PERSONALITY: Challenger

WORK STYLE: Insister, Asserter

LEADERSHIP: Director

RELATIONSHIPS: Challenging

COMMUNICATION: Blunt, direct

EIGHT WITH A SEVEN WING: More joyful, responsive, and extroverted

EIGHT WITH A NINE WING: More calm, relaxed, and receptive

BASIC FEAR: Out of control

BASIC DESIRE: Control, power

DRIVE: To show they are strong and resist vulnerability; to be in control and exercise strength; to rule their situation and environment

LOST IN CHILDHOOD: The world can be trusted

LEARNED IN CHILDHOOD: Don't trust, don't show weakness

NEED TO LEARN: Being vulnerable with God and with the appropriate people is the source of my true strength.

LOVING AN EIGHT requires time to build trust. Eights need a purposeful display of affection, even when they don't look like they need it. Many times they feel it is just them against the world, remind them with encouraging words that you believe in them and are in their corner. Tell them that they can trust you and why they can trust you. Help them to see when they are overbearing or dominating in their effect. Encourage them to be sensitive to the position of another that they feel is against them. Help them to get out of crusade mode by enjoying the play of children. Help Eights develop an appetite for experiences where they don't have to show their power.

SPIRITUAL PRACTICES FOR EIGHTS:
Confess self-reliance and lust and reclaim vulnerability and innocence
Learn how much force is necessary
Moderate impact on others
Appreciate others' truths
Practice compassion

SCRIPTURE MEDITATION:
True-self celebration

A father to the fatherless, a defender of widows, is God in his holy dwelling. God sets the lonely in families; he leads forth the prisoners with singing, but the rebellious live in a sun-scorched land. (Psalms 68:5–6)

SCRIPTURE MEMORY VERSE:
Inviting the false self to transformation

My grace is sufficient for you, for my strength is made perfect in weakness. Therefore, most gladly I will rather boast in my infirmities, that the power of Christ may rest upon me. (2 Corinthians 12:9)

BREATH PRAYER:
Your power is perfect in my weakness

GROWTH AND INTEGRATION:
Engage life-giving intellect of the 5: Hold all things loosely, observe, detach, and learn more about an issue before reacting.
Engage the life-giving heart of the 2: Empathy, compassion, and warmth.

TIPS FOR TYPES:
-Become acquainted with a quieter dimension of your life
-Experiment with your energy
-Practice relaxing your energy
-Let others in
-Enjoy without controlling

EIGHT PARABLES: Matthew 13:24–30 Wheat & Tares. Forcibly extract the evil.

EIGHT IN SCRIPTURE: Samson, Martha

Style Eight: The Powerful Person

I AM	I AM NOT	I AM	I AM NOT
strong	weak	passionate	ambivalent
powerful	impotent	energetic	phlegmatic
magnanimous	small	impulsive	procrastinator
self-sufficient	needy	hardworking	easygoing
independent	dependent	industrious	lazy
assertive	push-over	forceful	shy
confrontational	avoidant	intimidating	meek
challenging	wimp	aggressive	timid
revolutionary	slave	fearless	fearful
in charge	subordinate	hard	soft
in control	helpless	rough	smooth
my way	accommodating	tough	bleeding heart
boss	subservient	invincible	vulnerable

List derived from: Enneagram Spectrum Certification Program, Jerome Wagner, Ph.D.

Reflection Practice

In solitude and silence, ask God to help you be open and honest with yourself and God. Begin with breathing. Breathing in, "I am made in God's image," and then breathing out, "I am not God." Spend a few minutes with this breath prayer. Feel the goodness and freedom of being made in God's image. Feel the liberty of letting God be God.

Now, keep breathing and notice without judgment what emerges for you from the words on the list above using the questions below:

What word in the "I am not" list is the word to which you are most resistant? What might life look like if you opened up to that word/description as something positive or useful in others? In yourself?

What words in the "I am" list best describe you? Which word are you most attached to? Addicted to? Describes your false/compulsive self? If there is a sin pattern attached to this word, confess this to God and ask for forgiveness...receive God's forgiveness.

Now, with a spiritual friend ask each other a repeating question using one of those "I am" words. What would it mean to let go of the "I am" word that best describes you? Let this be a repeating question until you get to the root of what it would mean to let go of that description of you. See what happens.

Does this help you return to your TRUE self? Why or why not?

Spend time talking to God about what you are aware of, journaling, and talking with a spiritual friend.

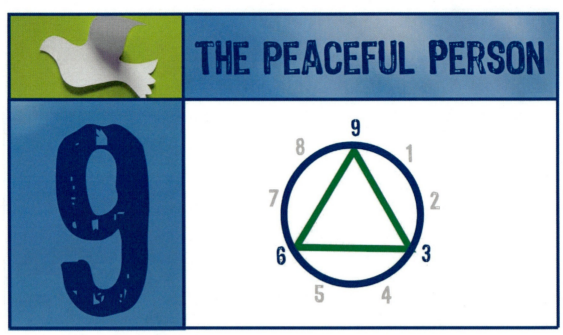

You will keep him in perfect peace, whose mind is stayed on You because he trusts in You. -- **Isaiah 26:3 (NKJV)**

TRUE SELF: The Peaceful Person. Nines show us that God is Peace. Nines are accepting, trusting, and stable. They are good-natured, kind-hearted, relaxed, and supportive. Transforming Nines are accepting and nonjudgmental, and they approach others with an embrace-all style. They practice conflict transformation for the good of all involved in a conflict. They are the easygoing, self-effacing type. They can merge with others and forget their agenda to create shared results. Nines who are present are comfortable in their skin and bring others the same grace. They are adaptable, compassionate, easygoing, supportive, patient, and nonjudgmental; they go with the flow. Unflappable Nines are self-effacing and working for effectual peace, engaged and using their energy to address conflict/peace issues. Transforming Nines are diplomatic, simply succeeding for the sake of others. Centered Nines embody Holy Harmony.

FALSE SELF: Non-transforming Nines can be indecisive, spaced-out, apathetic, undisciplined, unassertive, passive-aggressive, and stubborn. Unaware Nines are disconnected from their needs, feelings, and anger. They merge with others at the cost of their desires. They are stubborn and shut off from feelings. They lose themselves in the lives of others.

AUTHENTIC TRUE SELF: Peacemaker, Holy Harmony

COMPULSIVE FALSE SELF: Slothful

REDEMPTIVE VIRTUE BACK TO TRUE SELF: Action

PERSONALITY: Acceptor

WORK: Receptionist

LEADERSHIP: Mediator

RELATIONSHIPS: Accommodating

COMMUNICATION: Easygoing

NINE WITH AN EIGHT WING: more assertive, confrontational, and energetic

NINE WITH AN ONE WING: more objective, critical, and task oriented

BASIC FEAR: Of loss and separation

BASIC DESIRE: To have inner stability, hang loose, "peace of mind."

DRIVE: Avoid conflicts, have peace in the environment, preserve the status quo. No waves, no tension to resist whatever would upset or disturb harmony.

LOST IN CHILDHOOD: Your presence matters.

LEARNED IN CHILDHOOD: It's not okay to assert yourself.

NEED TO LEARN: "I make a difference, and I matter to God's purposes for the world."

LOVING A NINE requires respecting their individuality and asking them regularly about that. Find out what their needs, desires, and dreams are. See how you can support them in an accomplishment. Make space for them to do what they enjoy. Take the time to hear their opinion on a subject and employ their ideas. Encourage them to have a chance to live in their bodies through regular exercise or classes that develop the physical side of life. Encourage them to share what they are angry about regularly so they don't have a blow-up or melt-down.

SPIRITUAL PRACTICES FOR NINES:
Confess slothfulness and anger
Pay attention to own needs
Set own boundaries, limits, priorities
Love self as well as others
Accept conflict and discomfort as part of growth

SCRIPTURE MEDITATION:
True-self celebration

You will keep those in perfect peace, whose mind is stayed on you because they trust in you. (Isaiah 26:3)

SCRIPTURE MEMORY VERSE:
Inviting the false self to transformation

The kingdom of heaven has been forcefully advancing, and forceful people lay hold of it. (Matthew 11:12)

BREATH PRAYER:
Mighty God—Prince of Peace

GROWTH AND INTEGRATION:
Engage the life-giving heart of 3: Production, efficacy, and confidence.
Engage the life-giving intellect of 6: Loyalty, insight, and questioning.

TIPS FOR TYPES:
-Ask yourself what you need and want
-Develop a relationship with your body
-Take intentional, focused action on your priorities
-Learn about your anger

NINE PARABLES: Luke 14:16–24 (The Great Banquet) Called but asleep or busy with the lesser

NINE IN SCRIPTURE: Jonah, Abraham

Style Nine: The Peaceful Person

I AM	I AM NOT	I AM	I AM NOT
peaceful	frantic	noble plodding	quick
harmonious	hassled	unflappable	emotionally expressive
fair	biased	unexcitable	nervous
comfortable	edgy	stable	erratic
serene	driven	avoid conflict	conflicted
relaxed	energetic	patient	pushy
easy-going	ambitious	ecumenical	bigoted
balanced	imbalanced	inclusive	excluding
easy	aggressive	cool	hot-headed
laid back	Type A	uninvolved	passionate
calm	upset	uncommitted	decisive
accommodating	controlling	creature of habit	unpredictable

List derived from: Enneagram Spectrum Certification Program, Jerome Wagner, Ph.D.

Reflection Practice

In solitude and silence, *ask God to help you be open and honest with yourself and God. Begin with breathing. Breathing in, "I am made in God's image," and then breathing out, "I am not God." Spend a few minutes with this breath prayer. Feel the goodness and freedom of being made in God's image. Feel the liberty of letting God be God.*

Now, keep breathing and notice without judgment what emerges for you from the words on the list above using the questions below:

What word in the "I am not" list is the word to which you are most resistant? What might life look like if you opened up to that word/description as something positive or useful in others? In yourself?

What words in the "I am" list best describes you? Which word are you most attached to? Addicted to? Describes your false/compulsive self? If there is a sin pattern attached to this word, confess this to God and ask for forgiveness...receive God's forgiveness.

Now, with a spiritual friend *ask each other a repeating question using one of those "I am" words. What would it mean to let go of the "I am" word that best describes you? Let this be a repeating question until you get to the root of what it would mean to let go of that description of you. See what happens.*

Does this help you return to your TRUE self? Why or why not?

Spend time talking to God about what you are aware of, journaling, and talking with a spiritual friend.

God saw all that He had made, and it was very good. —Genesis 1:31

TRUE SELF: Healthy Ones show us God is good. Ones embody the goodness of God. Ones are self-disciplined, hardworking, organized, wise, discerning, realistic, noble, conscientious, and productive, as well as morally heroic. They embody the goodness of God. Transforming Ones are ethical but don't live by others "oughts" and "shoulds." They are principled and can reform what is wrong and make it right. Aware Ones are ethical and trustworthy and regulate that energy to serve rather than perfect. Ones are motivated by the need to live life well, including improving themselves and helping other people and the world around them. Integrated Ones are creative reformers who can joyfully say, *"it is good enough,"* and end the day. Sacred Crusaders.

FALSE SELF: Unaware Ones must live life the "right" way, including improving themselves, other people, and the world around them. They are meticulous to their own hurt. They are addicted to maintaining high standards. Their inner-critic demands another tweak or correction to make things perfect. Non-transforming Ones are afraid of making a mistake. They are picky, finicky, judgmental, and impatient. Ones have repressed anger as they view the world through their list of the oughts and shoulds, right and wrong judgments. Deforming Ones can be self-righteous, overly serious, hypercritical of themselves and others. They are rigid, inflexible, and controlling.

AUTHENTIC, TRUE SELF: Good

COMPULSIVE, FALSE SELF: Angry

REDEMPTIVE VIRTUE BACK TO TRUE SELF: Grace

PERSONALITY: Reformer, Perfecter

WORK STYLE: Quality Performer

RELATIONSHIPS: Moral

COMMUNICATION: What's right and correct

ONE WITH A NINE WING: Likely to be more peaceful, relaxed

ONE WITH A TWO WING: More caring, compassionate, and concerned for others

BASIC FEAR: Of being imperfect/defective

BASIC DESIRE: To be good and moral

DRIVE: Want to be right, to strive higher and improve everything, to be consistent with their ideals, to justify themselves, to be beyond criticism so as not to be condemned by anyone.

LEARNED IN CHILDHOOD: It's not okay to make mistakes.

LOST IN CHILDHOOD: You are good.

NEED TO LEARN: "It's not my responsibility to fix everything, only what God asks me to fix in the world."

LOVING A ONE takes appreciating that they have high standards and telling them so. You can show them by being on time and trying to keep things organized that affect them. Help them to give themselves a break. Schedule time with them for fun and relaxation. If you live with them, do your share of the work. Admit your mistakes and encourage them that they don't have to be perfect to be loved. Recognize when they are trying to reform you; it is done to help you. Allow them to suggest improvements. Gently assist them to accept the goal, embrace their humanity, not perfect it. Give them the space they need to be independent without feeling rejected. Encourage them to express their angry and imperfect feelings to you, without trying to sanitize it; this will help them tremendously.

SPIRITUAL PRACTICES FOR ONES:
Compassion for self
Recognize and confess the critical internal voice (the inner critic) regularly
Allow time to relax, play, and accept yourself and others as you/they are

SCRIPTURE MEDITATION;
True-self celebration

God saw all that he had made, and it was very good. (Genesis 1:3)

SCRIPTURE MEMORY VERSE:
Inviting the false self to transformation

"Why do you call me good?" Jesus answered. "No one is good except God alone." (Luke 18:19)

BREATH PRAYER:
God alone—is good.

GROWTH AND INTEGRATION:
Engage the life-giving intellect of 7: fun, optimism, and new ideas.
Engage the life-giving heart of the 4: authenticity, warmth, beauty in difficulty, and empathy.

TIPS FOR TYPES:
-Get to know your inner critic
-Give yourself and others a break
-Practice making mistakes
-Accept tenderness and caring
-Take care of yourself (but not as a "should")

ONE PARABLE: Luke 15:11–33 Extending compassion to others when you have kept all the rules.

ONE IN THE SCRIPTURE: Paul writing to the Galatians and the Romans. John the Baptizer

Style One: The Good Person

I AM	I AM NOT	I AM	I AM NOT
good (very)	bad	responsible	irresponsible
right	wrong	reliable	fair-weather friend
upright	licentious	dependable	undependable
moral	immoral	professional	amateur
righteous	unethical	committed	uninvolved
just	unjust	careful	careless
principled	law breaker	persistent	quitter
upstanding	loose	critical	tolerant
firm	wishy-washy	strict	forgiving
fair	arbitrary	opinionated	blind
ethical	unethical	organized	disorganized
idealistic	realistic	meticulous	impulsive
high standards	slip shod	thorough	haphazard
standard bearer	compromising	tidy	sloppy

*List derived from: Enneagram Spectrum Certification Program, Jerome Wagner, Ph.D.

Reflection Practice

In solitude and silence, ask God to help you be open and honest with yourself and God. Begin with breathing. Breathing in, "I am made in God's image," and then breathing out, "I am not God." Spend a few minutes with this breath prayer. Feel the goodness and freedom of being made in God's image. Feel the liberty of letting God be God.

Now, keep breathing and notice without judgment what emerges for you from the words on the list above using the questions below:

What word in the "I am not" list is the word to which you are most resistant? What might life look like if you opened up to that word/description as something positive or useful in others? In yourself?

What words in the "I am" list best describes you? Which word are you most attached to? Addicted to? Describes your false/compulsive self? If there is a sin pattern attached to this word, confess this to God and ask for forgiveness...receive God's forgiveness.

Now, with a spiritual friend ask each other a repeating question using one of those "I am" words. What would it mean to let go of the "I am" word that best describes you? Let this be a repeating question until you get to the root of what it would mean to let go of that description of you. See what happens.

Does this help you return to your TRUE self? Why or why not?

Spend time talking to God about what you are aware of, journaling, and talking with a spiritual friend.

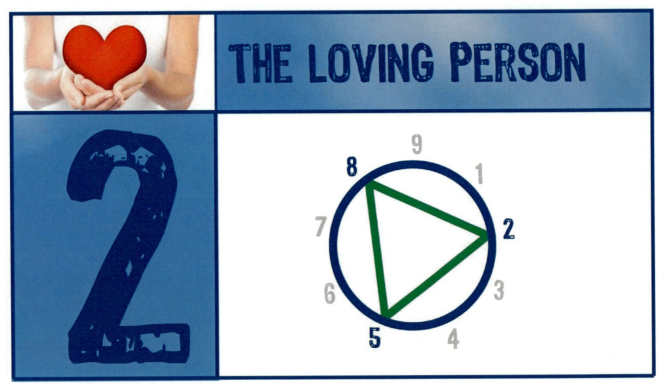

THE LOVING PERSON

For I was hungry and you gave me something to eat, I was thirsty and you gave me something to drink, I was a stranger and you invited me in... —Matthew 25:35

TRUE SELF: The Loving Person. Two's show us that God is love. Twos are the caring, interpersonal type. They are empathetic, sincere, and warm-hearted. They are friendly, generous, and self-sacrificing. Their attention naturally goes to others' needs and desires, but when aligned with Love, they can give the Divine while aware of their human limitations. They relate easily to people, enjoy giving to others, and are capable of unconditional love. Transforming Twos show strong care, measured helpfulness, detached service, and wise offerings. Aware Twos offer generous nurture where appropriate, aligned with respect for self and others. Centered Twos embody Divine Love.

FALSE SELF: Unhealthy Twos are proud of their giving, want to be indispensable, are boastful, and are manipulative in their giving—quid pro quo. Non-transforming Twos are clingy, indirect, and possessive. They are addicted to "loving" and proving that nobody can love you as they love you. No good deed goes uncalculated, and reciprocation is noted. Un-centered Twos are martyr-like, working way beyond your and their boundaries. They are insecure, vainglorious, and preoccupied with gaining approval.

AUTHENTIC, TRUE SELF: Loving

COMPULSIVE, FALSE SELF: Prideful

REDEMPTIVE VIRTUE BACK TO TRUE SELF: Humility

PERSONALITY: Carer

WORK STYLE: Helper

LEADERSHIP: Pleaser

RELATIONSHIPS: Helpful

COMMUNICATION: What's helpful and compassionate?

TWO WITH A ONE WING: Task oriented, idealistic, and judgmental.

TWO WITH A THREE WING: Gregarious, competitive, and project-focused.

BASIC FEAR: Of being rejected, unwanted, unloved

BASIC DESIRE: To be loved

DRIVE: Want to be loved, to express their feelings for others, to be needed and appreciated, to get others to respond to them, to vindicate their claims about themselves.

LOST IN CHILDHOOD: You are wanted.

LEARNED IN CHILDHOOD: It's not okay to have your own needs.

NEED TO LEARN: To ask myself, "What do I need?" ...and then ask for help from God and others.

LOVING A TWO requires appreciating their love by thanking them and encouraging them. Ask them whether physical touch, cards, gifts, or reassuring words are the best way to communicate your love and appreciation for them. Notice what their needs are and ask them to be honest with you about their real feelings. Be interested in their life and don't take advantage of the Two's willingness always to help you. Encourage them to use the word "NO" when they can't do something for you or others, then celebrate them for saying it. Help them set limits for their lives, for their emotional and physical health. Be gently honest with them when you feel they are possessive or clingy or when you sense they are trying to make you feel guilty.

SPIRITUAL PRACTICES FOR TWOS:
Confess impure motives for care
Learn to receive
Nurture a separate self
Pay attention to personal needs
Solitude and silence

SCRIPTURE MEDITATION:
True-self celebration

I was hungry and you gave me something to eat, I was thirsty and you gave me something to drink, I was a stranger and you invited me in, I needed clothes and you clothed me, I was sick and you looked after me, I was in prison and you came to visit me. Truly I tell you, whatever you did for one of the least of these brothers and sisters of mine, you did for me. (Matthew 25:35–36, 40)

SCRIPTURE MEMORY VERSE:
Inviting the false self to transformation

But we have this treasure in jars of clay to show that this all-surpassing power is from God and not from us. (2 Corinthians 4:7)

BREATH PRAYER:
Power is from God—not from me.

GROWTH AND INTEGRATION:
Engage the life-giving instincts of 8: decisive, confident, and direct.
Engage the life-giving intellect of 5: observant, detached, and wise.

TIPS FOR TYPES:
- Practice showing your love for others by simply being with them
- Create a practice for developing a clear, quiet mind
- Find support for opening your heart to yourself
- What is it you need? Who do you need it from?
- Experiment with nurturing yourself

TWO PARABLE: Luke 14:7–11. The place of honor at the marriage feast and motivation for servanthood.

TWO IN SCRIPTURE: John the Beloved, Ruth, and Boaz

Style Two: The Loving Person

I AM	I AM NOT	I AM	I AM NOT
helpful	selfish	empathetic	uncaring
needed	needy	sympathetic	heartless
indispensable	useless	sensitive	indifferent
generous	petty	thoughtful	thoughtless
caring	uncaring	considerate	inconsiderate
supportive	destructive	responsive	unresponsive
nurturing	violent	ready	unconcerned
loving	hateful	feeling	cold
lovable	angry	intuitive	insensitive
peaceful	aggressive	observant	unaware
caretaking	neglectful	attentive	inattentive
serving	stingy	warm	cold
self-sacrificing	self-centered	hospitable	unwelcoming
altruistic	self-absorbed	friendly	alone

*List derived from: Enneagram Spectrum Certification Program, Jerome Wagner, Ph.D.

Reflection Practice

In solitude and silence, ask God to help you be open and honest with yourself and God. Begin with breathing. Breathing in, "I am made in God's image," and then breathing out, "I am not God." Spend a few minutes with this breath prayer. Feel the goodness and freedom of being made in God's image. Feel the liberty of letting God be God.

Now, keep breathing and notice without judgment what emerges for you from the words on the list above using the questions below:

What word in the "I am not" list is the word to which you are most resistant? What might life look like if you opened up to that word/description as something positive or useful in others? In yourself?

What words in the "I am" list best describes you? Which word are you most attached to? Addicted to? Describes your false/compulsive self? If there is a sin pattern attached to this word confess this to God and ask for forgiveness...receive God's forgiveness.

With a spiritual friend ask each other a repeating question using one of the "I am" words. What would it mean to let go of the "I am" word that best describes you? Let this be a repeating question until you get to the root of what it would mean to let go of that description of you. See what happens.

Does this help you return to your TRUE self? Why or why not?

Spend time talking to God about what you are aware of, journaling, and talking with a spiritual friend.

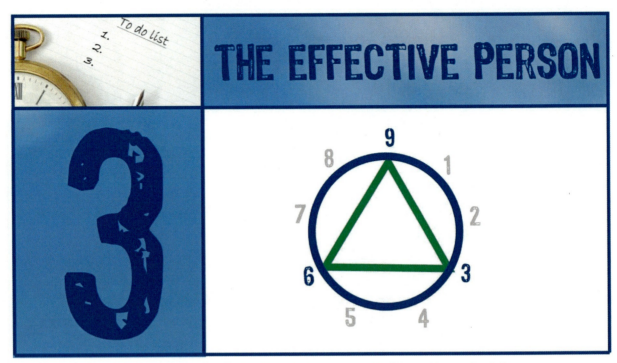

THE EFFECTIVE PERSON

God said, "Let there be light," and there was light. —Genesis 1:3

TRUE SELF: Threes show us God is effective. Threes are the adaptable, achievement-oriented type. Threes are self-assured, magnetic, ambitious, competent, and energetic. They make good leaders who motivate others to live up to their potential. As an action-oriented high performer, their energy, competence, and optimism impart confidence to others. Transforming Threes reproduce from intimacy with God rather than manufacturing a product from workaholism. Aware Threes are authentic in everything they do; they are role models who inspire others. Transforming Threes show humble competence, servant leadership, and empowering presence. They display harmonized energy and authentic affections. Centered Threes embody Sacred Confidence.

FALSE SELF: Driven Threes are addicted to the need to be productive, inspiring, motivational, efficacious, admired, and successful at whatever they do. They can become addicted to tasks and things to accomplish. Workaholism, image management, and competitiveness are the compulsions of the Three. "Cutting corners" and "whatever-it-takes" work modes lead to the Three's self-deception. When trapped in the "achieve more" mode, they disconnect with their deeper feelings and lose connection with themselves and others. When driven by performance, they become more of a human doing than a human being.

AUTHENTIC, TRUE SELF: Effective, Achieving

COMPULSIVE, FALSE SELF: Deceitful

REDEMPTIVE VIRTUE BACK TO TRUE SELF: Truth

PERSONALITY: Efficacious

WORK STYLE: Producer

LEADERSHIP: Motivator

RELATIONSHIPS: Task oriented

COMMUNICATION: Energetic, assertive

THREE WITH A TWO WING: Collaborative, friendly, and concerned for others

THREE WITH A FOUR WING: Creative, responsive, and shows more feelings

BASIC FEAR: Of being worthless

BASIC DESIRE: To feel valuable and worthwhile

DRIVE: Want to be affirmed, to distinguish themselves from others, to have success, to be admired, and to impress others

LOST IN CHILDHOOD: You are loved for yourself.

LEARNED IN CHILDHOOD: It's not okay to have your own feelings and identity.

NEED TO LEARN: How other people see me is none of my business; how God sees me is my business.

LOVING A THREE requires someone who can help them slow down and enjoy life. Let them know you love them not for their accomplishments but just for being who they are. Help them to set limits and boundaries for their work. Make space for them or encourage them to support their inner life, not just the work of the outer world. Help them to pay attention to their feelings and allow them to express them honestly. Don't disturb them or feel rejected by them when they are very busy. Join them in their work to help lighten the load, but be honest with them if you see they have taken on more than is humanly possible. Acknowledge and celebrate their achievements/successes, even though they don't look like they need it or anything else from you.

SPIRITUAL PRACTICES FOR THREES:
Solitude and silence
Practice the spiritual discipline of slowing
Confess deceit and fear of failure
Pay attention to own needs

SCRIPTURE MEDITATION:
Celebrating the true self

And God said, "Let there be light," and there was light. (Genesis 1:3)

SCRIPTURE MEMORY VERSE:
Inviting the false self to transformation

All have sinned and fallen short of the glory of God. (Romans 3:23)

BREATH PRAYER:
All have sinned—I fall short

GROWTH AND INTEGRATION:
Engage the life-giving instincts of 9: peace, harmony, and self-forgetfulness.
Engage the life-giving intellect of 6: loyalty, insight, and questioning.

TIPS FOR TYPES:
-Practice sharing your real self with others
-Pay attention to your heart
-Practice asking, "What is true about this situation?"
-Create time and space that is just for you without any need to perform
-Be curious about the urge to succeed at any price

THREES PARABLES Matthew 20:20–23 One on the right, one on left. Wife (and sons) of Zebedee and the addiction to success.

THREES IN SCRIPTURE: Jacob, Saul, David

Style Three: The Effective Person

I AM	I AM NOT	I AM	I AM NOT
successful	failure	leader	follower
productive	inactive	winner	flop
efficient	inefficient	networker	drifter
competent	incompetent	savvy	naïve
capable	incapable	smooth	sticky; tacky
accomplished	indolent	popular	unpopular
organized	disorganized	attractive	nerdy
get things done	time-waster	looking good	slob
fast	lethargic	confident	diffident
promoter	wait and see	self-assured	loser
salesperson	sit on shelf	sociable	shy
bottom line	bogged down	hard worker	lazy

*List derived from: Enneagram Spectrum Certification Program, Jerome Wagner, Ph.D.

Reflection Practice

In solitude and silence, *ask God to help you be open and honest with yourself and God. Begin with breathing. Breathing in, "I am made in God's image," and then breathing out, "I am not God." Spend a few minutes with this breath prayer. Feel the goodness and freedom of being made in God's image. Feel the liberty of letting God be God.*

Now, keep breathing, and notice without judgment what emerges for you from the words on the list above using the questions below:

What word in the "I am not" list is the word to which you are most resistant? What might life look like if you opened up to that word/description as something positive or useful in others? In yourself?

What words in the "I am" list best describes you? Which word are you most attached to? Addicted to? Describes your false/compulsive self? If there is a sin pattern attached to this word, confess this to God and ask for forgiveness...receive God's forgiveness.

Now, with a spiritual friend *ask each other a repeating question using one of those "I am" words. What would it mean to let go of the "I am" word that best describes you? Let this be a repeating question until you get to the root of what it would mean to let go of that description of you. See what happens.*

Does this help you return to your TRUE self? Why or why not?

Spend time talking to God about what you are aware of, journaling, and talking with a spiritual friend.

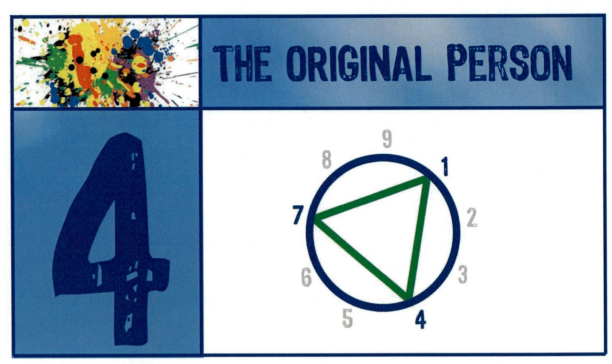

*He has made everything beautiful in its time.
He has also set eternity in the hearts of men; yet they cannot fathom
what God has done from beginning to end.* —Ecclesiastes 3:11–12

TRUE SELF: Fours show us God is Original. Fours are self-aware, sensitive, and they offer beauty and creative energy. They are authentic, self- revealing, emotionally honest, and personal. They are not afraid to live in the beauty, celebration, tragedy and grief of life. Fours are primarily motivated by the need to understand and express their cavernous feelings. They long to discover what is authentic in themselves. Transforming Fours intentionally use their highly developed imagination, creativity, inspiration, and authenticity to renew themselves and restore others. Healthy Fours show us that God is Creator. They are imaginative, sensitive, intuitive, creative, and artistic. Centered Fours allow the height and depth of their souls to be used as gifts to lead others to self-awareness. Fours embody Sacred Awe and Mystery.

FALSE SELF: Unaware Fours withhold themselves from others due to feeling vulnerable and defective. Fours on their edge focus on whatever is missing, distant, and dreamed. They can get lost in love with the world of romance, fantasy, and imagination. The drive to feel special and unique, but their need to avoid being seen as ordinary robs them of presence. Non-transforming Fours can also feel contemptuous and exempt from ordinary ways of living. Un-centered Fours have problems with self-indulgence, hypersensitivity, worthlessness, idealism, depression, and self-loathing.

AUTHENTIC TRUE SELF: Creative

COMPULSIVE FALSE SELF: Envious

REDEMPTIVE VIRTUE BACK TO TRUE SELF: Equanimity

PERSONALITY: Creator

WORK STYLE: Expressionist

LEADERSHIP: Personalist

RELATIONSHIPS: Approach-Withdrawal

COMMUNICATION: Dramatic

BASIC FEAR: Insignificance

BASIC DESIRE: Uniqueness, significance

FOUR WITH A THREE WING: more efficient, active, and enterprising

FOUR WITH A FIVE WING: more logical, detached, and analytical

DRIVE: Connection and isolation. Express feelings and moods, create feelings and moods in others.

LOST IN CHILDHOOD: You are seen for who you are.

LEARNED IN CHILDHOOD: It's not okay to be too functional or too happy.

NEED TO LEARN: The beauty and purpose of my life are based on the small, ordinary events that God provides.

LOVING A FOUR requires accepting that what feels like drama to you is their absolute truth. Be present to their pain as well as their descriptions of beauty. See them. Hear them. Enter into their world. Encourage them to find an outlet for their imagination in writing, painting, dancing, cooking, decorating, or any art form that expresses the depth of their emotions and offers something life-giving. Be honest with them when they want to run because something is missing. Help them find what to be grateful for and what is present and ordinary. Help them to recognize when they are in a withdrawal/pursuit cycle.

SPIRITUAL PRACTICES FOR FOURS:
Confess envy and desire for what isn't
Focus on what is positive in the present
Be consistent in action despite fluctuating and intense feelings
Appreciate the ordinary

SCRIPTURE MEDITATION:
True-self celebration

He has made everything beautiful in its time. He has also set eternity in the hearts of men; yet they cannot fathom what God has done from beginning to end. (Ecclesiastes 3:11–12)

SCRIPTURE MEMORY VERSE:
Inviting the false self to transformation

A sound heart is the life of the flesh but envy the rottenness of the bones. (Proverbs 14:30)

BREATH PRAYER:
I am grateful—for the present moment

GROWTH & INTEGRATION:
Engage the life-giving instincts of 1: objectivity, stability, and self-discipline
Engage the life-giving intellect of 7: optimism, joy, and spontaneity

TIPS FOR TYPES:
-Develop a relationship with your body
-Acknowledge your actual gifts and talents
-Become interested in and engaged with others
-Recognize feelings for what they are

FOUR PARABLES: Matthew 6:25–30. Be anxious for nothing. You already have what you need.

FOUR in Scripture: Job, Mary Magdalene

Style Four: The Original Person

I AM	I AM NOT	I AM	I AM NOT
original	copy	exciting	boring
different	dull	unpredictable	routine
creative	unimaginative	lonely	gregarious
special	typical	elite	trendy
extraordinary	ordinary	classy	tasteless
remarkable	mundane	stylish	off-the-rack
unique	banal	flamboyant	common
intuitive	obtuse; linear	refined	rough
empathetic	insensitive	sophisticated	boorish
imaginative	literal-minded	tasteful	tacky

*List derived from: Enneagram Spectrum Certification Program, Jerome Wagner, Ph.D.

Reflection Practice

In solitude and silence, ask God to help you be open and honest with yourself and God. Begin with breathing. Breathing in, "I am made in God's image," and then breathing out, "I am not God." Spend a few minutes with this breath prayer. Feel the goodness and freedom of being made in God's image. Feel the liberty of letting God be God.

Now, keep breathing and notice without judgment what emerges for you from the words on the list above using the questions below:

What word in the "I am not" list is the word to which you are most resistant? What might life look like if you opened up to that word/description as something positive or useful in others? In yourself?

What words in the "I am" list best describes you? Which word are you most attached to? Addicted to? Describes your false/compulsive self? If there is a sin pattern attached to this word, confess this to God and ask for forgiveness... receive God's forgiveness.

Now, with a spiritual friend ask each other a repeating question using one of those "I am" words. What would it mean to let go of the "I am" word that best describes you? Let this be a repeating question until you get to the root of what it would mean to let go of that description of you. See what happens.

Does this help you return to your TRUE self? Why or why not?

Spend time talking to God about what you are aware of, journaling, and talking with a spiritual friend.

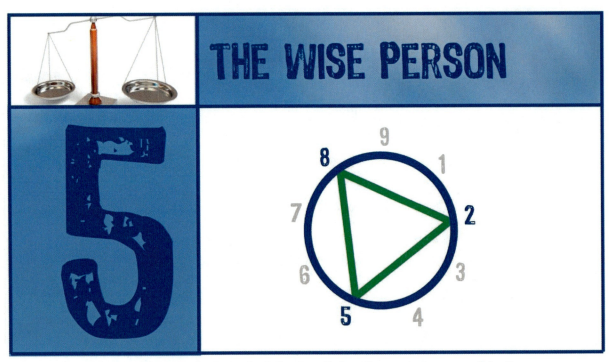

*For who has known the mind of the Lord that he may instruct him?
But we have the mind of Christ.* —1 Corinthians 2:16

TRUE SELF: Healthy Fives show us God is Wisdom. They are objective, focused, calm, perceptive, insightful, and curious. Fives are the intense, cerebral type. Fives are alert, insightful, and curious. They are individualistic. Fives are motivated by the need to gain knowledge and to be independent and self-sufficient, and healthy Fives use that knowledge in magnanimous ways. Transforming Fives are futurists, visionaries, and innovators who are at home with complex ideas. Fives can use their skills of observation and experimentation for the good of humanity. Their bounty of knowledge can be shared. Centered Fives embody generous wisdom—Holy Wisdom.

FALSE SELF: Fives can be intellectually arrogant, withholding, controlled, cynical, negative, standoffish, and stingy. Un-centered fives are addicted to distance and detachment. They guard their privacy and space and avoid being engulfed by others. Unhealthy Fives become preoccupied with their thoughts and imaginary constructs. Fear can keep them attached to thinking and unable to access feelings. When on their edge they are intense and highly anxious. They are plagued with meaninglessness and gather more information or protection to allay their fears.

AUTHENTIC TRUE SELF: Wise

COMPULSIVE FALSE SELF: Greedy

REDEMPTIVE VIRTUE BACK TO TRUE SELF: Detachment

PERSONALITY: Observer

WORK STYLE: Thinker

LEADERSHIP: Systematizer

RELATIONSHIPS: Intellectual

COMMUNICATION: Ideas and theories

FIVE WITH A FOUR WING: more sensitive, intuitive, and connected to feelings

FIVE WITH A SIX WING: more likely to be committed, dutiful, and connected to a group

BASIC FEAR: Incompetence, incapability

BASIC DESIRE: Competence, capability

DRIVE: To watch, know, analyze, understand, and ultimately figure things out intellectually as a way to secure.

LOST IN CHILDHOOD: It's okay to be comfortable in the world.

LEARNED IN CHILDHOOD: It's okay to have needs.

I NEED TO LEARN: It is safe to be in the world because God has me connected to God's self and the people in the world.

LOVING A FIVE requires understanding that they are not interested in meaningless talk. Let them tell you about something that interests them even the last little detail of it. Respect their privacy and allow for it. Ask them about what is going on in their feeling world by letting them use an image, song, or color and then help them expound on that. Suggest they take a class that encourages their creativity or use of their bodies, and consider doing it with them. Admire them and their competencies, and encourage them to share those with the wider world.

SPIRITUAL PRACTICES FOR FIVES:
Confess withholding wisdom from others
Take a creative course to engage your body and emotions
Choose ways to engage with groups that can benefit from your loving wisdom

SCRIPTURE MEDITATION:
True-self celebration

For who has known the mind of the Lord that he may instruct him? But we have the mind of Christ. (1 Corinthians 2:16)

SCRIPTURE MEMORY VERSE:
Inviting the false self to transformation

Wicked borrows and never returns; Righteous gives and gives. Generous gets it all in the end; Stingy is cut off at the pass. (Psalm 37:21 MSG)

BREATH PRAYER:
God gives wisdom—I share God.

GROWTH AND INTEGRATION:
Engage life-giving instincts of 8: Confident action, leadership, and direct communication.
Engage the heart of 2: Empathy, compassion, and warmth.

TIPS FOR TYPES:
-Notice what you ignore in life
-Begin to enjoy the experience of inner knowing in contrast to having mental knowledge
-Allow yourself to observe the tendency to buy the belief that you are separate from the rest of the world
-Find your body and awaken it with movement
-Use breath prayer/scripture meditation to quiet the mind

FIVE PARABLE: Matthew 14:13-21. Feeding of five thousand. When you share, everyone can get enough.

FIVE IN SCRIPTURE: Joseph, Nicodemus

Style Five: The Wise Person

I AM	I AM NOT	I AM	I AM NOT
wise	foolish	good listener	intrusive
perceptive	naïve; simplistic	thorough	unprepared
astute	stupid	whole picture	myopic
witty	dull	synthesizing	trivializing
aware	oblivious	analyzer	flaky
observant	manipulatable	undemonstrative	feeling
curious	unaware	contained	effusive
contemplative	in action	reserved	flamboyant
mystic	simplistic	serious	silly
studious	unreflective	pedantic	entertaining

*List derived from: Enneagram Spectrum Certification Program, Jerome Wagner, Ph.D.

Reflection Practice

In solitude and silence, ask God to help you be open and honest with yourself and God. Begin with breathing. Breathing in, "I am made in God's image," and then breathing out, "I am not God." Spend a few minutes with this breath prayer. Feel the goodness and freedom of being made in God's image. Feel the liberty of letting God be God.

Now, keep breathing and notice without judgment what emerges for you from the words on the list above using the questions below:

What word in the "I am not" list is the word to which you are most resistant? What might life look like if you opened up to that word/description as something positive or useful in others? In yourself?

What word in the "I am" list best describes you? Which word are you most attached to? Addicted to? Describes your false/compulsive self? If there is a sin pattern attached to this word confess this to God and ask for forgiveness... receive God's forgiveness.

Now, with a spiritual friend ask each other a repeating question using one of those "I am" words. What would it mean to let go of the "I am" word that best describes you? Let this be a repeating question until you get to the root of what it would mean to let go of that description of you. See what happens.

Does this help you return to your TRUE self? Why or why not?

Spend time talking to God about what you are aware of, journaling, and talking with a spiritual friend.

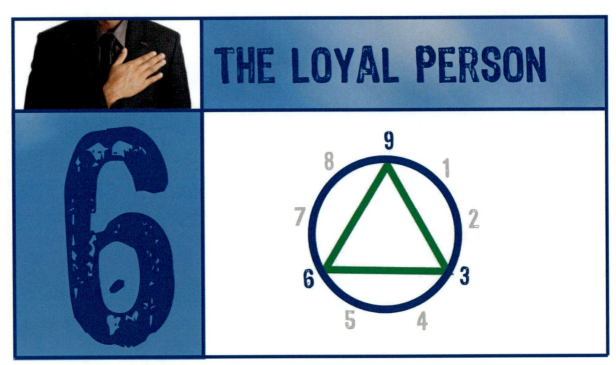

THE LOYAL PERSON

The steadfast love of the LORD never ceases; his mercies never come to an end; they are new every morning; great is thy faithfulness.
—**Lamentations 3:22-23**

TRUE SELF: Sixes show us God is Faithful. Transforming Sixes are reliable, hardworking, and responsible. They show us holistic trustworthiness, responsible relinquishment, non-anxious vigilance, and peaceful questioning. Sixes look for danger and potential threats and anticipate where trouble or danger might arise. They are awake and ask insightful questions. They are trustworthy, responsible, alert, loyal, compassionate, and sympathetic to underdog causes. Centered Sixes are faithful participants in the organizations they serve. Sixes embody Sacred Vigilance.

FALSE SELF: Un-centered Sixes are motivated by the need to feel secure and in control, to have safety and predictability. Feeling a sense of belonging and finding someone trustworthy to depend on is an addiction for a Six. Unhealthy Sixes withdraw to protect themselves ("phobic") and/or confront fearful situations head-on, even seeking them out ("counter-phobic"). Sixes are relentless in getting what they want. Non-transforming Sixes fixate on hazards and worst-case scenarios and how to deal with them. They are often cautious and indecisive, operating from self-doubt and suspicion. Overly reactive and defiant., they can be defensive, rebellious, and highly anxious, running on stress while complaining about it.

AUTHENTIC TRUE SELF: Loyal

COMPULSIVE FALSE SELF: Fearful

REDEMPTIVE VIRTUE BACK TO TRUE SELF: Courage

PERSONALITY: Joiner

WORK STYLE: Relater

LEADERSHIP: Teamster

RELATIONSHIPS: Loyal

COMMUNICATION: Agreeable, dutiful

SIX WITH A FIVE WING: more introverted, intellectual and cautious

SIX WITH A SEVEN WING: more playful, spontaneous and innovative

BASIC FEAR: Insecurity

BASIC DESIRE: Security

DRIVE: Want to have security, to feel supported by others, to have certitude and reassurance, to test the attitudes of others toward them, to fight against anxiety and insecurity.

LEARNED IN CHILDHOOD: It's not okay to trust yourself.

LOST IN CHILDHOOD: You are safe.

NEED TO LEARN: My security lies within my relationship with God.

LOVING A SIX requires understanding that fear that is imagined is real fear. Help them become present to their anxiety and explore it with them to determine if it has any real merit. Help them learn to identify with what makes them fearful or over-reactive. Appreciate their loyalty by respecting it and not abusing it. Be sure to have time to talk about how you feel about one another to bring assurance in the relationship. When you see them operating in self-doubt, remind them of their goodness and worthiness.

SPIRITUAL PRACTICES FOR SIXES:
Confess fear and ask for faith
Accept insecurity as part of life
Recognize that flight/fight are reactions to fear and develop new strategies to deal with fear
Get to know people you don't agree with, understand, or fear

SCRIPTURE MEDITATION:
True-self celebration

The steadfast love of the LORD never ceases, his mercies never come to an end; they are new every morning; great is thy faithfulness. (Lamentations 3:22–23)

SCRIPTURE MEMORY VERSE:
Inviting the false self to transformation

There is no fear in love. But perfect love drives out fear because fear has to do with punishment. The one who fears is not made perfect in love. (1 John 4:18)

BREATH PRAYER:
Your perfect love—drives out fear.

GROWTH AND INTEGRATION:
Engage the life-giving instincts of 9: peace and harmony.
Engage the life-giving heart of 3: production, efficacy, and confidence.

TIPS FOR TYPES:
-Quiet your mind
-Acknowledge fear, befriend courage
-Acknowledge your inner authority
-Acknowledge the insight that has been made available to you
-Look for the positive aspects of a situation

SIXES IN PARABLES: Luke 19:11–28 Parable of treasure. Fear can paralyze leaders and talents.

SIXES in Scripture: Timothy and Peter

Style Six: The Loyal Person

I AM	**I AM NOT**	**I AM**	**I AM NOT**
loyal	disloyal	hospitable	rude
devoted	traitorous	warm	cool
faithful	treacherous	kind	mean
responsible	irresponsible	friendly	unfriendly
trustworthy	rebellious	communal	isolated
dependable	undependable	cooperative	difficult
dutiful	fickle	vigilant	negligent
true blue	mixed bag	awake	lights out
enduring	flaky	fearful	relaxed
persistent	flighty	prudent	reckless
obedient	disobedient	careful	careless

List derived from: Enneagram Spectrum Certification Program, Jerome Wagner, Ph.D.

Reflection Practice

In solitude and silence, ask God to help you be open and honest with yourself and God. Begin with breathing. Breathing in, "I am made in God's image," and then breathing out, "I am not God." Spend a few minutes with this breath prayer. Feel the goodness and freedom of being made in God's image. Feel the liberty of letting God be God.

Now, keep breathing and notice without judgment what emerges for you from the words on the list above using the questions below:

What word in the "I am not" list is the word that you are most resistant to? What might life look like if you opened up to that word/description as something positive or useful in others? In yourself?

What words in the "I am" list best describes you? Which word are you most attached to? Addicted to? Describes your false/compulsive self? If there is a sin pattern attached to this word confess this to God and ask for forgiveness...receive God's forgiveness.

Now, with a spiritual friend ask each other a repeating question using one of those "I am" words. What would it mean if I let go of _____ (the "I am" word that best describes you). Let this be a repeating question until you get to the root of what it would mean to let go of that description of you. See what happens.

Does this help you return to your TRUE self? Why or why not?

Spend time talking to God about what you are aware of, journaling, and talking with a spiritual friend.

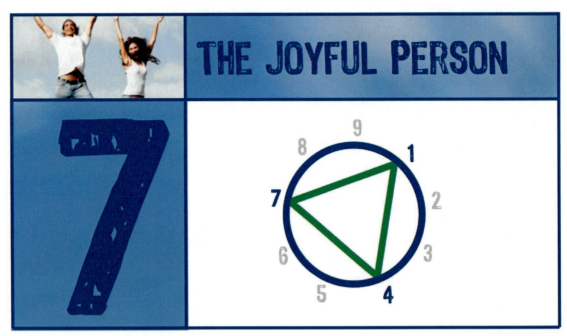

Go and enjoy choice food and sweet drinks, and send some to those who have nothing prepared. This day is sacred to our Lord. Do not grieve, for the joy of the LORD is your strength. —Nehemiah 8:10

TRUE SELF: The Joyful Person. Centered Sevens show us that God is Joy. Sevens are versatile, optimistic, spontaneous, playful, high-spirited, and practical. They seek new and exciting experiences that bring life to themselves and others. Healthy Sevens are visionaries who focus their talents on worthwhile goals. Transforming Sevens are joyous, highly accomplished, and full of gratitude. Centered Sevens discover that joy includes living in the mundane and even tragedy. They accept life as an adventure, yet they also want to be grounded with what is most important. Sevens embody Sacred Joy.

FALSE SELF: Sevens are addicted to the need to be happy and stay busy, keeping their options open, keeping life "up," including compulsively making plans for new experiences. Non-transforming Sevens are overextended, scattered, undisciplined, distracted, and exhausted by staying on the go. Un-centered Sevens have problems with superficiality and impulsiveness. Boredom, suffering, painful emotions and the everyday drudgeries of life must be avoided at all costs. Sevens on their edge are self-centered, insensitive, narcissistic, hyperactive, and undisciplined, and they can have problems with completion and long-term commitments.

AUTHENTIC TRUE SELF: Joyful

COMPULSIVE FALSE SELF: Gluttonous

REDEMPTIVE VIRTUE BACK TO TRUE SELF: Sobriety

PERSONALITY: Cheerer

WORK STYLE: Animator

LEADERSHIP: Cheerleader

RELATIONSHIPS: Social

COMMUNICATION: Enthusiasm, stories, humor

SEVEN WITH A SIX WING: "The Entertainer," more moderate, persistent, attentive to duty

SEVEN WITH AN EIGHT WING: "The Realist," more aggressive, competitive and controlling

BASIC FEAR: Pain and deprival

BASIC DESIRE: Satisfaction, fulfillment

KEY MOTIVATIONS: Want to avoid missing out on an adventure. Desire freedom, interesting and exciting experiences. Reject pain and boredom. Need to be occupied.

LOST CHILDHOOD MESSAGE: You will be taken care of.

LEARNED CHILDHOOD MESSAGE: It's not okay to depend on anyone for anything.

NEED TO LEARN: Fulfillment exists in experiencing the beauty of what God gives in the here and now.

LOVING A SEVEN is an invitation to take part in the adventure. Celebrate their ability to see what you cannot see. Enjoy their enthusiasm. Help them to be at peace with life's pain. Support strategic action to deal with difficult issues. Help them to find love and satisfaction in the present moment. Help them name feelings and stay with those feelings. Empower them or give them the space to get out of the stimulation of life and learn to appreciate silence and solitude. Help them to stop planning the future and be in the here and now.

SPIRITUAL PRACTICES FOR SEVENS:
Let go of plans
Live simply. Try minimalism
Confess self-indulgence, addiction to positivity, and seeing only the positive
Make and fulfill commitments

Wherever you are, be all there
Learn to become more aware of others
Allow pain and uncomfortable emotions to be your teachers

SCRIPTURE MEDITATION;
True-self celebration

Go and enjoy choice food and sweet drinks, and send some to those who have nothing prepared. This day is sacred to our Lord. Do not grieve, for the joy of the LORD is your strength. (Nehemiah 8:10)

SCRIPTURE MEMORY VERSE:
Inviting the false self to transformation

Those who sow in tears will reap with songs of joy. (Psalm 126:5)

BREATH PRAYER:
A man of sorrows—acquainted with grief.

GROWTH AND INTEGRATION:
Engage the life-giving instincts of 1: principled, disciplined, organized, and present. Engage the life-giving heart of 4: reflective, authentic, and able to enter into difficulty.

TIPS FOR TYPES:
-Quiet your mind
-Practice a new way to schedule, allowing extra buffer time
-Experience and stay with feelings
-Enjoy what is here now
-Give yourself a chance to develop your full capabilities

SEVENS IN PARABLES: Mark 8:31–33, Jesus prophesies His suffering.
The trance of compulsive optimism and the avoidance of pain

SEVENS in Scripture: Woman at the Well, Solomon

Style Seven: The Joyful Person

I AM	I AM NOT	I AM	I AM NOT
joyful	joyless	ingénue	jaded
fun	serious	youthful	old
happy	sad	whimsical	routine
free	rigid	energetic	lethargic
spontaneous	predictable	animated	expressionless
enthusiastic	dull	active	passive
stimulating	boring	action-taking	static
bubbly	flat	alert	asleep
playful	workaholic	exciting	bland
funny	solemn	interesting	tedious
witty	humorless	multi-talented	one-dimensional
quick-witted	slow	friendly	hostile

*List derived from: Enneagram Spectrum Certification Program, Jerome Wagner, Ph.D.

Reflection Practice

In solitude and silence, *ask God to help you be open and honest with yourself and God. Begin with breathing. Breathing in, "I am made in God's image," and then breathing out, "I am not God." Spend a few minutes with this breath prayer. Feel the goodness and freedom of being made in God's image. Feel the liberty of letting God be God.*

Now, keep breathing and notice without judgment what emerges for you from the words on the list above using the questions below:

What word in the "I am not" list is the word to which you are most resistant? What might life look like if you opened up to that word/description as something positive or useful in others? In yourself?

What word in the "I am" list best describes you? Which word are you most attached to? Addicted to? Describes your false/compulsive self? If there is a sin pattern attached to this word confess this to God and ask for forgiveness...receive God's forgiveness.

Now, with a spiritual friend *ask each other a repeating question using one of those "I am" words. What would it mean to let go of the "I am" word that best describes you? Let this be a repeating question until you get to the root of what it would mean to let go of that description of you. See what happens.*

Does this help you return to your TRUE self? Why or why not?

Spend time talking to God about what you are aware of, journaling, and talking with a spiritual friend.

PRESENCE AND NON-PRESENCE: A REFLECTION EXCERCISE

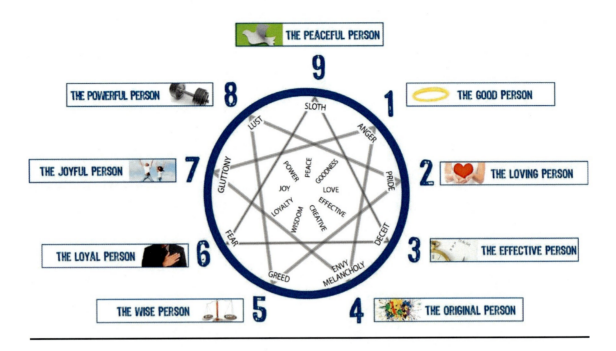

Being present to the Presence of God is what the Enneagram is all about. Let's say it this way "be present to Presence." When you are not present to your true self, you are not in Presence. Not only are you not showing up but you also rob yourself and everyone else of your true Presence and the Presence of God. The Enneagram shows us how to return to our true selves. One little alliteration can help us be aware.

> *Ones- position and perfection keep us from Presence*
> *Twos – people pleasing and possessiveness keep us from Presence*
> *Threes – performance and pragmatism keep us from Presence*
> *Fours – personalizing and pouting keep us from Presence*
> *Fives – pontificating and privatizing keep us from Presence*
> *Sixes – paranoia and pledging keep us from Presence*
> *Sevens – playing and preoccupation keep us from Presence*
> *Eights – powering up and prosecuting keep us from Presence*
> *Nines – powering down and procrastinating keep us from Presence*

Being aware our Triad motivation and fixation can help us detach from it. Our Triad will determine where we start from most of the time.

GQ – Gut Triad or Gut Center (8,9,1)
Core Motivation: power and control
Negative Fixation: anger and guilt
Narrative: "I've had enough" or "I haven't done enough."

IQ – Head Triad or Head Center (5,6,7)
Core Motivation: security and survival
Negative Fixation: fear and anxiety
Narrative: "I won't have enough. I'll get what I need."

EQ – Heart Triad or Heart Center (2,3,4)
Core Motivation: approval and affection
Negative Fixation: shame and fear of humiliation
Narrative: "I am not enough. I must prove I am."

In addition to **core motivation and negative fixation**, all nine types have a **defense mechanism.** *When unaware of our defense mechanisms, we will be at their service, on our edge, functioning in false-self mode and away from Presence.*

*These things must be noticed in a prayerful position. Read the **"Notice without judgement"** questions for your type all the way through and decide how you would like to proceed. If you are not being guided on retreat or with a spiritual companion, ask the questions on your voice memo and have them read to you.*

Prayer Posture: *Place yourself in an open and receptive position. Legs uncrossed, feet flat on the ground, hands open or gently connected, and back straight. If you have back problems, try with your back on the ground and calves on a chair. Maybe walking or standing is best for you. Once you are comfortable, take a deep breath. Give thanks that you are alive and God is with you here. Keep breathing and listen to the questions. Listen once all the way through without responding. Then with your journal or out loud (maybe with a friend) listen to your story, "noticing without judgment."*

- **Eights' Defense Mechanism:** *Denial.* Denial is the refusal to accept reality or fact, acting as if a painful event, thought, or feeling did not exist.

Notice without judgment. *When do I react without thinking? When have I ignored tenderness and vulnerability in the heat of the moment? When have power and control dismissed cool-headed and warmhearted responses? How is anger showing up? Where did anger show up saying, "I have done enough"? When has guilt shown up saying, "I haven't done enough"? What is happening in my body as I notice and name these moments? What is my earliest memory of this feeling? What might that tell me?*

- **Nines' Defense Mechanism:** *Narcotization.* Narcotization is using food, drink, entertainment, or repetitive patterns of thinking and doing to "put oneself to sleep."

Notice without judgment. *When have I just done what someone else wanted without paying attention to my own desire? When did real priorities get set aside for something/someone else? When has stubbornness kept me stuck? What am I angry about? Where did anger show up saying, "I have done enough"? When has guilt shown up saying, "I haven't done enough"? How am I responding to discomfort, stress, and* *conflict? What is happening in my body right now? What is my earliest memory of this feeling? What might that tell me?*

- **Ones' Defense Mechanism:** ***Reaction Formation***. Reaction formation is feeling one thing but expressing the opposite to control emotion.

Notice without judgment. *When have I judged what is right and wrong, who is good and who is bad? When have I scolded myself? When have I compared myself? Where did anger show up saying, "I have done enough"? When has guilt shown up saying, "I haven't done enough"? What is my inner critic saying to me these days? What happens in my body as I ask these questions? What is my earliest memory of this feeling? What might that tell me?*

- **Twos' Defense Mechanism:** ***Repression***. Repression is suppressing "unacceptable" feelings and converting them into a more acceptable form of emotional energy.

Notice without judgment. *How has my, "You need me" or "I am indispensable" been showing up? When have I been superficial, lying, and using flattery? What happens when I notice my own vainglory? Where do I see humility in my life? What do I need now? Who do I need to support me? Have I told them I need their support? What happens in my body as I ask these questions? What is my earliest memory of this feeling? What might that tell me?*

- **Threes' Defense Mechanism:** ***Identification***. Identification means taking on a role so completely that we lose contact with who we are inside.

Notice without judgment. *How have I been living in "fake it to make it" mode? Where am I managing my image? How have I lost myself in a role, task, or a job? Do I feel like a human doing or a human being? When am I using deceit? What are my feelings? What am I feeling right now? Am I aware of shame? Where is fear of humiliation showing up? What happens in my body as I ask these questions? What is my earliest memory of this feeling? What might that tell me?*

- **Fours' Defense Mechanism:** ***Introjection***. Introjection is unconsciously incorporating the characteristics of a person or object into one's own psyche.

Notice without judgment. *Where do I express arrogance? How is envy showing up? What ordinary things am I ignoring or dismissing? What is missing from my life right now? Who or what do I envy? Who is misunderstanding me? What is shame saying to me? Where is the fear of humiliation showing up? Who doesn't know I'm special? What or who is telling me I am not enough? Where am I proving I am enough? What happens in my body as I ask these questions? What is my earliest memory of this feeling? What might that tell me?*

- **Fives' Defense Mechanism: *Isolation*.** Isolation can be physical withdrawal from others but also means staying in the head and withdrawing from one's emotions.

Notice without judgment. *Who have I been stingy with? What am I withholding from others? Why? When did I isolate myself physically to avoid contact with someone? When did I retreat into my head so as not to feel my feelings? When did I get stuck in analyzing or systematizing and lose sight of people? How am I minimizing desire? How am I ignoring a feeling? Who am I ignoring that is evoking emotion in me? Why don't I think I have enough? What am I striving to get no matter what it costs? What is happening in my body as I consider these questions? What is my earliest memory of this feeling? What might that tell me?*

Sixes' Defense Mechanism: *Projection*. Projection is attributing inner concerns and fears to others and external situations.

Notice without judgment. *Who have I projected my feelings onto? What situation has grown larger in my mind? What internal dialogue has incessant doubt and questioning attached to it? What decision am I afraid to make? What am I afraid of or anxious about? What am I alarmed about? Are these questions holding me back? Why don't I think I have enough? What am I striving to get no matter what it costs? What is happening in my body as I consider these questions? What is my earliest memory of this feeling? What might that tell me?*

- **Sevens' Defense Mechanism: *Rationalization*.** Rationalization is staying in the head or explaining away or justifying feelings and behaviors in order to avoid accepting responsibility or pain.

Notice without judgment. *Whose feelings and needs am I forgetting about? What pain am I avoiding? How are my ideas and plans distracting me from what is important to me? What activities or planning for the future am I using to avoid pain or negative feelings? How does reframing what's happening keep me from what is true and necessary? How are new options and possibilities hurting me and the people I care about? Why don't I think I have enough? What am I striving to get no matter what it costs? What is happening in my body as I consider these questions? What is my earliest memory of this feeling? What might that tell me?*

PSALM 139 TRUE SELF/FALSE SELF REFLECTIONS

Read the passage slowly and reflectively. Underline the word(s) that emerge, shine, convict, provoke, call for attention, or capture you.

1 You have searched me, Lord, and you know me.
2 You know when I sit and when I rise; you perceive my thoughts from afar.
3 You discern my going out and my lying down; you are familiar with all my ways.
4 Before a word is on my tongue you, Lord, know it completely.
5 You hem me in behind and before, and you lay your hand upon me.
6 Such knowledge is too wonderful for me, too lofty for me to attain.
7 Where can I go from your Spirit? Where can I flee from your presence?
8 If I go up to the heavens, you are there;
if I make my bed in the depths, you are there.
9 If I rise on the wings of the dawn, if I settle on the far side of the sea,
10 even there your hand will guide me, your right hand will hold me fast.
11 If I say, "Surely the darkness will hide me and the light become night around me,"
12 even the darkness will not be dark to you; the night will shine like the day,
for darkness is as light to you. 13 For you created my inmost being;
you knit me together in my mother's womb.
14 I praise you because I am fearfully and wonderfully made; your works are wonderful, I know that full well.
15 My frame was not hidden from you when I was made in the secret place,
when I was woven together in the depths of the earth.
16 Your eyes saw my unformed body;
all the days ordained for me were written in your book
before one of them came to be.
17 How precious to me are your thoughts, O God! How vast is the sum of them!
18 Were I to count them, they would outnumber the grains of sand—
when I awake, I am still with you.
19 If only you, God, would slay the wicked!
Away from me, you who are bloodthirsty!
20 They speak of you with evil intent;
your adversaries misuse your name. 21 Do I not hate those who hate you, Lord,
and abhor those who are in rebellion against you?
22 I have nothing but hatred for them; I count them my enemies.
23 Search me, God, and know my heart;
test me and know my anxious thoughts.
24 See if there is any offensive way in me,
and lead me in the way everlasting.

Notice – Hold the word or words that asked for your attention. Write them down. When you feel ready, set them aside for now and...

Say to God – *"I praise you because I am fearfully and wonderfully made; your works are wonderful, I know that full well."*

Ask yourself – "When or how am I aware that I am living from my True Self, made in the image of God Self?" Take time to stay with that awareness. Celebrate with God times and places you have seen your life in God, living out *"the days ordained for me were written in your book."*

When you feel ready – Together with God allow a search: *"Search me, O God, and know my heart; Try me and know my anxious thoughts; and see if there be any hurtful way in me, and lead me in the everlasting way."*

When or how am I aware of my False Self? When am I aware that I am away from God's will and plan for my life? How do I see my vulnerability to sin increase when living in false-self patterns? What "anxious and hurtful ways" do I need to talk to God about?

Confess – "*Let us lay aside every weight, and the sin which doth **so easily beset us**, and let us run with patience the race that is set before us*" (Hebrews 12:1 KJV). Ask God to forgive you, Jesus to cleanse you, and the Holy Spirit to enable you to be free to run your race.

Receive – *"If we confess our sins, He is faithful and righteous to forgive us our sins, and to cleanse us from all unrighteousness"* (1 John 1:9 ASB).

Receive that God is the faithful and righteous one, and you are not. Rest in God's forgiveness. Know that God longs to be gracious to you. Confession opens us up to the grace of awareness. Awareness opens us to the grace of transformation.

Return to your first reflections – See if the words you received in the reflective reading have something to say to you now. Take time to listen to God and your heart. Have a conversation with God and let God love you.

REST: *"Yet the LORD longs to be gracious to you; therefore He will rise up to show you compassion. For the LORD is a God of justice. Blessed are all who wait for Him!"* (Isaiah 30:18)

SPIRITUAL PRACTICE OF TRANSFORMATION

*"I have met the enemy and the enemy is me" can describe the way we can sabotage our lives either through self-hatred or pride. If we operate in self-aggrandizement and grandiosity **or** self-loathing and low self-esteem, we are living below the idea God had, which is to live in His Image and likeness. Transformation is the biblical way to bring our caterpillar-like self to the state of the beautiful butterfly.*

Images of Transformation to ponder
Gems being polished by friction
Gold being purified by fire
Ice melting into water
A caterpillar becoming a butterfly
A child forming in the womb

Exercises to practice attentiveness to transformation
Take a walk. Look for images that are pictures of transformation. Let the Holy Spirit speak to you. Journal what you see.

or

Sit quietly. Allow images of transformation from scripture to come to you about transformation, e.g., Saul to Paul; Moses the murderer to Moses the deliverer; The thirsty Samaritan woman to the first documented female Evangelist. What did they live through that brought transformation? List those things.

or

Listen to different kinds of music. What does it do to your body (gut center)? How does it affect your thoughts (head center) or emotions (heart center)? What does that teach you about transformation? What does it tell you about you?

Where does God want to transform me?

How can I be more confident? How can I be more humble?

How can I be more assertive? How can I be more yielding?

***"No longer be conformed to the pattern of this world
but be transformed by the renewing of your mind" (Romans 12:2)***

REFLECTIONS
WITH A SPIRITUAL FRIEND

Remember that you are made in the image and likeness of God. The space you most identify with is God's way of bringing that part of God's self to the world.

Take time for silence and choose someone to lead this prayer.

Father, we are fearfully and wonderfully made. Give us the ability to celebrate ourselves and each other as we share our thoughts about ourselves. With your help we shall become ourselves, the selves that you love and want to love the world through. Amen.

Let each one share their thoughts as they are ready. Take one question at a time.

How does the Enneagram description fit you? Are you surprised by what you saw? Are the descriptions and traits consistent with what you already knew about yourself?

Name what you are grateful for about yourself. Your friend/spouse?

Name what is difficult to know about yourself.

What are the gifts and goodness that I see in myself that is like God? How can I give that to my friend/spouse? To the wider world?

What would be a scripture that could encourage you toward transformation of your false self? What would be a scripture that would celebrate God's love for your true self, made in God's image?

How can you grow into your true/healthy self?

What can you let go of in your false/unhealthy self that you see as destructive?

ENNEAGRAM COURSES and CERTIFICATION PROGRAM

ENNEAGRAM COURSES *for individuals, churches, businesses, and nonprofits*

The Enneagram Personality Styles: A Tool for Self-Knowledge and Spiritual Transformation
Services-
4–8-hour Workshop
2-day Retreat
Individual Spiritual Direction, Consulting, or Training

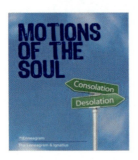

Motions of the Soul:© iEnneagram
Services
4–8-hour Workshop
2-day Retreat
Individual Spiritual Direction, Consulting, or Training

For fee schedule, contact: cl@ccmonline.org
Prices are negotiable for small churches and nonprofit organizations.

CERTIFICATION: MOTIONS OF THE SOUL ©iENNEAGRAM PRACTITIONER
4-Day Training and Certification

WHAT YOU WILL TAKE AWAY
2 Unique Enneagram Guides and PowerPoint presentations by Clare Loughrige:
- ©***The Enneagram Personality Styles: A Tool for Self-Knowledge and Spiritual Transformation***
- ©Enneagram Personality Styles, 80+ slides
- ©***Motions of the Soul: The Enneagram Meets Ignatius, The©iEnneagram***
- ©Motions of the Soul: ©iEnneagram, 80+ slides

TRAINING INCLUDES
- Christian historical roots of the Enneagram
- The basic theoretical framework on which the Enneagram is based
- Understanding nine Enneagram styles
- Harmony Triads Theory, Ramon Lull's 14th-century diagram
- Trinitarian theory
- Deep knowledge of yourself and what developed that self
- Defense mechanisms and ego fixation awareness practices
- True-Self/False-Self awareness and tools to choose life and wholeness
- Ignatian spiritual practices that inform the ©iEnneagram
- Spiritual Disciplines to center each style
- Spiritual Rhythms for interior freedom
- Practices to develop a whole and discerning life
- Learning to interpret Enneagram test results

WHO WILL BENEFIT FROM THIS TRAINING?
Therapists; counselors; spiritual directors; coaches; consultants; managers; human resource personnel; pastors; teachers; anyone interested in personal development; spiritual formation and transformation; and persons wishing to expand their knowledge of the Enneagram to improve their work and personal relationships will benefit from this training.

WHAT TO EXPECT
A dynamic, edifying, informative teaching from an International Enneagram Association Professional, First Analysis Institute Teacher, and Aspell Empowerment Enterprises Practitioner (see bio and recommendations). Training includes interaction and contemplation.

CHOOSE FROM MULTIPLE TRAINING DATES
Visit:
ScottAndClareLoughrige.org and click on "**©iEnneagram Training/Certification**" for upcoming dates and information.

WHERE
Crossroads Church – **Marshall, MI**

LOCAL LODGING
Holiday Inn, Hampton Inn Marshall. Hotels are 2 blocks from the Crossroads.

Prerequisite
*Wagner Enneagram Personality Style Scales wepss.com
Participants will take the only Enneagram inventory published by a major psychological test company with sufficient research to be reviewed in the Buros Center's Mental Measurements Yearbook. **Cost $10.00**

*Participants will take this Inventory and learn to interpret the results
MOS:©iEnneagram-style.

Certification Requirement Questions

What are the requirements for Certification besides attending the training?
- Creating a workshop outline with material during training.
- Developing Head, Heart, Gut Motion Mantras (based on curriculum) for each type.
- Working through the spiritual practices, writing and processing with your head, heart, and gut types during retreat and alone in evenings.
- Enneagram head, heart, gut type (autobiography) reflection. To be completed within one month after training.

Is your program suitable for all levels of Enneagram knowledge (beginning through advanced)?

Yes! Takeaways will vary with experience. But participants will receive certification specific to their core competencies (determined in the post-training application) in the Enneagram and spiritual formation education and experience.

Two levels of certification:
- Professional Certification
- Certificate of Completion

CONTACT CLARE LOUGHRIGE

cl@ccmonline.org

SOURCES AND RESOURCES

Enneagram Spectrum of Personality, Dr. Jerome Wagner

The Enneagram Discernment of Spirits, Audio version Fr. Richard Rohr

The Enneagram: A Christian Perspective, Fr. Richard Rohr, Andreas Ebert

Enneagram Spectrum of Personality, Dr. Jerome Wagner

Enneagram Psychology, Patrick Aspell PH.D., and Dee Dee Aspell M.A.

The Enneagram Personality Portraits: Enhancing Professional Relationships, Patrick and Dee Dee Aspell

The Essential Enneagram, David Daniels, M.D., Virginia Price, PH.D.

Invitation to Solitude and Silence, Ruth Haley-Barton, D.D.

Sacred Rhythms, Ruth Haley Barton, D.D.

Spiritual Disciplines Handbook, Practices That Transform Us, Adele Ahlberg Calhoun

Spiritual Disciplines For The Enneagram, Adele and Doug Calhoun, Clare and Scott Loughrige

Websites:
enneagramspectrum.com
enneagraminstitute.com (Daily Enneathought)

Enneagram Testing- wepss.com

I am deeply indebted to the many spiritual mothers, fathers, authors, and teachers of the Enneagram. This material has its origin and continuance through many centuries of voices that cannot be specifically attributed.

© *The Enneagram Personality Styles: A Tool for Self-Knowledge and Spiritual Transformation*
Clare Loughrige 2016. First Printing, 2007 All Rights Reserved
Because this material is original and some of it is used with the permission of other sources, do not make copies of this material without permission from the author.

Made in the USA
Middletown, DE
23 April 2024

53361254R00038